the mentor's mentor

Preparing Yourself to Make a Lasting Difference in Someone's Life

Corey Olynik

"...a great model to guide you through this seemingly
simple, but in reality, very complex relationship."
*From the Foreword by Ole Carlson,
author of Beneath the Armor*

The Mentor's Mentor

All enquires regarding this publication and Corey Olynik's speaking engagements to be made to:

CMO Strategies Inc.
900, 602 – 12th Avenue SW
Calgary, Alberta
T2R 1J3
info@coreyolynik.com

Refer to back pages for more information concerning the author, Corey Olynik

Editor: Catherine Nanton
Artwork and Graphics: Rod Schulhauser
Author Photograph: Roy Alexander
Printed in Canada by Motivated Publishing Ventures

ISBN

Acknowledgements

The story of a book is the story of a journey, of a life. While I will not name everyone, I must thank those who have had the biggest impact.

Thank you to the gang of **TEC-219** (The Executive Committee). It has been an honour to be your Chair for all these years. It's been my privilege to grow alongside you. Thank you my friends: Verne Cornwell, Al Gordon, George Goulet, Peter Kuelker, Dennis Little, Craig Matthews, Trevor Nimegeers, Garry Perry, Peter Smed and Pat Sullivan. You've allowed me into your lives and we're all better for it.

Thank you to the **TEC** tribe, especially those from whom I've learned the most: Ole Carlson, Rick Martin, James Newton, Garry Reuben, Susan Scott and Jim Motroni. You led me into myself and some amazing and unexpected discoveries.

Thank you to my **TEC** Chair colleagues and support here in Calgary: Doug Bouey, Dave Holte, Vera Colville, Phil Paxton, Mac Bourassa and Mary Bull. You remind me regularly that who I am matches what I do.

Thank you to Doug Whelpton and Dayle Medgett who encouraged me to organize and present this material to their lay leaders at **Westview Baptist Church**.

Thank you to Dan Reinhardt and the **CREST** leadership program for letting me refine my ideas with them.

Thank you to **Executive Directions** where I practice what I preach every day. I love you all. You make me feel valuable, each of you: Barbara Andrews, Denise Blair, Mark Brunton, Susan Cress, Walter Hosli, Penny Hume, Janet Lane, Wendy Lowe, Doug MacDonald, Gael MacLeod, Anoush Newman, Brian Pearson, John Rook, Bev Schecter and Karen Whiteman.

And to those bosses, mentors, teachers and teammates who have shaped me, thank you: Larry Schneider, Staff Barootes, Doug and Gord Rawlinson, Dennis Fisher, Alf Bentley, Grant Devine, Lloyd Avram, John Malach, Peter Matthews, Bruce

Haskins, Lewis Drummond, Marvin Tate, David Mueller, Jim Lockington, Cora Geddes, Penny Braaten, and Henry Kutarna.

Thank you to my editor, Catherine Nanton. You are the greatest. You have midwifed my ideas; they live! Without your efforts *The Mentor's Mentor* would still be a dream.

Thank you to Rod Schulhauser at **Motivated Publishing Ventures**. You've given me a chance. And you added some much needed discipline.

With deep gratitude I thank Wayne Stewart who has helped me believe in myself.

And from my heart, I thank my wife Kathee, who has always believed in me. Your love means everything. Everything.

To God be the glory.

Corey Olynik
April, 2006

Foreword by Ole Carlson
Author of *Beneath the Armor*

"You may not be aware of this, but Ole has a special gift." I overheard Corey Olynik speaking to my new bride, Sue Ann, at a dinner party wrapping up a two-day seminar I'd conducted in Tucson, AZ. I thought to myself, *I hope he doesn't have any pictures.* This was the second time Corey shared what he felt was his absolute truth about me. The first time I modestly brushed him off with a dismissing "Aw shucks, I don't know what you are talking about, but tell me more and please take your time." It is a risky proposition telling people that they have a gift. Gifts aren't always good things to have: such as a "gift of gab" or perhaps "looking a gift horse in the mouth" or taking "gifts from strangers." But somehow I felt that Corey's comments were meant to be a compliment, something that I that would make me proud.

Now that I have read his book, **The Mentor's Mentor**, I understand what he was saying that hot September night: my gift, in Corey's eyes, is that I am a natural mentor. What's surprising is I had no idea until I came across the description of an effective mentor he presents in this book. The only certainty I had regarding mentoring is that what I do, if anything, is mostly intuitive, and Corey makes that a legitimate base-camp for being a great mentor. Maybe it explains why my stated mission is "to influence those who InfluenceMany™." Perhaps Corey was mentoring me and I was unaware.

I often wondered why this intelligent, seemingly successful, energetic Canadian business executive kept showing up at seminars that I was conducting from Calgary to San Diego to Atlanta to Tucson. I'd look at the roster prior to the session and there it would be once again...**Corey Olynik...Calgary, Alberta**...and I'd think to myself *"he's back and I don't know why. Maybe I am a lousy teacher and he's not getting it."* Now I understand. I was one of his mentors without asking to be or consciously realizing it.

Well this is all very flattering but...Corey has some answers for you I never considered and a definitive roadmap to follow I never conceived. Should you choose mentoring as a profession or stumble into it as a volunteer, when you get involved in somebody's life (with permission) you can certainly use his great model to guide through this seemingly simple but in reality very complex relationship. Talk about being multi-faceted.

If it matters at all, I agree with most everything he says. Most importantly I want to emphasize the need for passion to mentor at an elevated, effective level. Both you and your protégé deserve it. Without passion or trusting your intuition, mentoring turns into a mechanical relationship with too many flowcharts, passages, milestones to reach and steps to remember. The recent influx of "wannabe" coaches and mentors, armed with crisp catalogue diplomas and mail-order certificates, is frustrating as it leaves a confused consumer with diluted, seemingly undifferentiated choices. That's sad.

Ahh, the bright side. Since you have opened this book you must have a serious personal or professional interest in mentoring. Don't settle. Take each chapter seriously, do the exercises, stretch yourself, put yourself in the shoes of the mentor, engage fully in the dialogue, and put your own spin on it. Be authentic within the framework in these pages. Corey suggests it is the **being** that really creates an extraordinary **doing**. You cannot fail from that position. Just keep in mind, please, always, the person across from you.

Ole Carlson

TABLE OF CONTENTS

Dear Journal:

Today I had a remarkable experience - one I never expected and that took me entirely by surprise. Andy has asked me to mentor him.

At first, I thought he was kidding - joking, teasing, making fun of our relationship - after all, I've got at least ten years on him, and he's always called me the dinosaur. But when I joked back, he insisted. He wants me to teach him what I know about being successful. Ha! That's a good one! What do I know about being successful? I'm just feeling my way like everyone else.

Andy tells me I've always been a role model for him, someone he wants to emulate. He wants me to coach him as he moves into position for promotion. I don't know the first thing about coaching, and I told him so. I said I'd think about it and let him know. We're meeting tomorrow.

So now, I'm thinking about it, and there's a lot to ponder.

Here I am, 40-something, just reaching a point where I actually know where I'm headed, and I'm not sure I know how I got here.

How will I know what to tell Andy? And what if I mess it up?

Introduction

"Hey Corey, I don't know if I've ever really thanked you enough for what you've been doing for me. It seems like every time we talk I feel more confident. I stare down things I haven't acknowledged before and I feel challenged to become even more than I used to think possible."

That felt great when I heard it. Little did I know that Doug's next few words would start me on a journey I wasn't expecting.

"You really know what you're doing. Hmmm," he said. *Oh no, I thought.* "Would you present a workshop on this whole area of mentoring, perhaps spend a Saturday with my team of volunteer leaders and help them learn the finer points?

What? Me? An expert?

I've always had trouble saying "No." Without thinking, I replied, "why not?"

That was the first step of my journey to becoming a *mentor's mentor.*

Both Doug and I knew how helpful it would be to have a framework to guide new mentors. The question was: could I make sense of the hundreds of disconnected thoughts and experiences floating around in my brain? What if I put some organization to those ideas? And what if someone actually found them useful?

I spent the next few days wondering why I'd said "yes" and what wisdom I might have developed. Honestly, I had been mentoring mentors in a number of different places for years, drawing on my own experience of helping hungry people hoping to grow.

Everyone has something that thrills them to the core. Personally, I love being in the room when someone's lights go on. I love throwing the switch. And I love that the light usually appears at that moment when neither of us expect it.

So I took Doug's challenge. I presented the workshop. And I fell in love with the process. I found a way to describe a mentor. I found a way to talk about how a mentor thinks. And I found a way to share what works for me without turning good ideas into rules or formulae. This book is what works for me. These are the ideas that wake me up in the morning.

Mentoring is not just a collection of fancy techniques and trusted catchphrases. Simply, mentoring is two people working in tandem to intentionally accelerate the growth of one. Mentoring is more than process, more than a series of meetings, more than the conversations they share; mentoring is a relationship. One does not *do mentoring* to another, one walks with someone arm in arm, helping them see and grow.

Mentoring is a way of being. Being is relationship. Relationship is dialogue. Being, relationship, and dialogue are largely intuitive. Intuition is like the wind. You can feel it but you can't see it. Nobody can describe it to you. Unless you've experienced it, you have no idea what it is or how it works.

So how does one put a framework to something that is, by my definition, intuitive? At first I wasn't sure I even should! I can give you a compass point, somewhere to take your bearings from, to give you directions – but I can't draw you a map.

This book will succeed if it informs your intuitive, rather than gives you a checklist. I want the concept of the mentoring relationship to wash over you, to immerse you, to soak in, to be absorbed until your actions and responses become second nature, and you walk by instinct. I want it to be like walking through your home in the dark. You are so familiar with the space you live in. You know where the furniture is, where the doorways are. If you know where you want to go you can find your way instinctively without even a stubbed toe. That's mentoring – moving confidently through the dark.

To do that, you have to sharpen your instincts. Fine-tune your antennae to discern the subtleties in these important conversations. To sense, rather than see or hear the message that's being conveyed. To intuit what's in behind his language, his doubts and his dreams.

And you have to be confident in your abilities, your ears and your questions; your confidence is the rock on which your protégé will stand. (There are many words to describe the "person being mentored:" pbm, learner, protégé, mentee. None are perfect. I've chosen to use "protégé" as it brings with it the feeling of "becoming more" that matters so much to me.)

This book is a how-to manual with a twist. I've intended it to speak to the mentor's character and technique by delving deeply into the six roles that every mentor must play at some time during the relationship.

Every mentor must be, first and foremost, a "Confidante:" a person who listens without judgment, who hears his protégé fully, openly and honestly.

Secondly, the mentor is usually chosen because she is a "Role Model" with some relevant experience that, if relayed effectively, will provide a positive influence to the protégé's development.

As a "Guide," a "Tutor," and a "Coach," the mentor leads the protégé into herself and facilitates growth.

The "Guide" walks alongside the protégé, showing the landmarks on the way, enlightening the protégé as to how to see them for herself.

The "Tutor" facilitates learning. When the protégé needs to know something, the mentor finds the most effective way to provide it.

The "Coach" brings accountability, discipline and motivation to the relationship.

The overarching role a mentor plays is that of "Sage:" the person who keeps his eye on the goal, the end result, the protégé's ultimate vision.

Simply put, this model builds on the notion that mentoring comes from within. Each mentor must have a passion for the growth of her protégé; she must share in the celebration of successes, she needs to feel the pain of setback and failure. Mentors need to train their instinct to know when to play each of the six roles, how to shift from one to another, and what to expect during the transition.

So this is my model. Read it, use it, tear it apart and put it back together again. Manipulate and massage it until it fits you perfectly. And wear the role proudly, knowing that you have a genuine impact on someone's life. Every successful person has someone to thank. Why not let it be you?

Dear Journal:

I met with Andy today, and I agreed to partner with him - the word mentor sounds so formal and scary, full of responsibility. Partner is so much easier; more relaxed, more like being on a journey together. And that's what we're doing - taking a journey on a path I've walked a few times myself.

It's not like I have to know everything. I only have to know a little bit more than Andy, right? Most of the stuff he's going through now I've already been through. That means I know the pleasures of doing things right and the pitfalls of doing the right thing. Surely I can communicate that to Andy in a way that he understands and can apply.

After all, mentoring is really just an ongoing conversation. He tells me what he's thinking. I ask him some questions to cause him to think outside the box he's created for himself. He responds with what's familiar to him. I come back with a different frame around the picture, expanding his thought network, stretching his imagination and creativity, lifting him up to a higher plane where the perspective is entirely different.

Really, Andy knows everything he needs to know to make his journey. I'm just there for him to ask questions out loud so he can hear the answers. He wants a sounding board to bounce ideas off.

"I wonder what would happen if..."

"What if we did it this way?"

"I don't think that would work, but if it was possible, how would I do it?"

And how much more will I learn, just seeing the world through Andy's eyes?

Chapter 1

One Conversation Many Installments

My mother was a music teacher. As a youngster, many days I would return from school to find a stranger playing the big piano in our dining room. She was also an accompanist – playing the piano for choirs, singers and instrumentalists in concerts and competitions. Way back then, she told me the secret to being a good accompanist is to be invisible to the audience, providing a stable foundation for the performer. In fact, a job well done provides depth and dynamic range underneath the performance that makes the soloist shine.

That's what drives successful mentors. We support someone and we remain unseen, releasing the protégé to make the music he or she is capable of making.

Personally, while I want to be an effective accompanist, eventually I want my protégé to sing a capella to the underlying music in his head, soaring to the possibilities in himself.

Repeat after me the accompanist's creed – now the mentor's creed – "It's not about me!"

In Homer's *Odyssey,* the hero Odysseus was compelled to leave his home to fight the Trojan War. He left his palace and his son Telemachus, under the care of his faithful friend Mentor, charging Mentor with the responsibility of raising his son to be an honourable, truthful and courageous man. Leaving out the myriad of typical Greek tragedy twists, Telemachus grew into the fine leader that made his father proud when he returned two decades later.

This is the source of the modern use of the word, mentor: *a trusted friend, counselor or teacher, usually a more experienced person.*

You have opened this book having come to a place where you are embarking on a mentoring journey, and you yourself are looking for guidance. Congratulations on reaching a place of experience and wisdom – at least a place where someone else thinks you know what you're doing! It's curious, isn't it? How we can reach a place where we think, "I wonder what to do next?" and just at that moment, someone comes to us for advice on the very thing we're questioning ourselves about? And in the giving of advice, we find the answer to our own conundrum?

Mentoring is not a checklist of dos and don'ts. At its core, mentoring is a relationship, an extended conversation between two people that intentionally accelerates the growth of one.

Mentoring is not just what's done when the two individuals meet; it is the essence of the two as a pair. Mentoring is more than process; it is relationship. One does not *do mentoring* to another. One walks with someone, rubbing up against them, helping them see and grow. That's the focus: mentoring is about growth. It's about walking with someone to help her reach her potential. It's about helping someone to become more than she would otherwise become, quicker. Mentoring is about bringing out the best in someone, not about creating what you want her to or think she should be.

Mentoring is a long conversation – asking questions, making assertions, following tangents and discovering principles and practices. Mentoring is a way of *being*, not a way of *doing*. After all, we are human "be"ings. And it is in our way of being that the protégé is first drawn to ask us for guidance. It's not our performance or accomplishments that make us the desired resource. It is who we are while we are performing and accomplishing. It is the values we demonstrate, the character we display, the compassion others experience that invite people to join with us.

What Do True Mentors Do?

A mentor's dream, to revisit the music metaphor, is for the protégé to be effective *a capella* – to fly on her own, to sing her own song, to make her own music, the music she was born to play or sing. Like jazz – you want your protégé to play the instrument that she is, released and free, rather than to just read the notes. Her soul and spirit are released.

A mentor holds up a mirror for his protégé – helps him to see who he is, see his possibilities, his gifts, his greatness. A mentor focuses on strength and not weakness. A mentor identifies potential and creates momentum. A mentor puts aside his own agenda to help his protégé express his own unique talents. A mentor accepts the protégé for who he is now, and sees the potential of who he can be.

I once read a story about some chickens in a chicken coop. A bunch of eggs hatched, and the chicks that pushed their way out grew up scratching around in the dirt, just like their mother hen taught them. One bird, scratching for his food, kept looking up into the sky as birds flew overhead, and felt a longing to fly with them. But he told himself, "Chickens don't fly." His friend encouraged him, saying, "Hey, maybe you're not a chicken. You sure don't look like me. You don't sound like me. Look at the size of your wings, man! I'll bet you could fly with those wings. Why don't you try?" Still the bird scratched around, and still he kept looking at the sky, until one day he saw a majestic eagle flying above the yard, calling its distinctive call, and he felt a longing he couldn't suppress. Suddenly, he started running through the yard, beating his wings. His friend cheered him on, and to his surprise, he lifted off and soared into the air, joined the eagle and found his true place in the sky.

A mentor doesn't have to embody the goals of the person she is mentoring. A mentor merely has to be able to see potential and find the right way of encouraging a protégé. Even a chicken can mentor an eagle.

A mentor's job is to find inside his protégé the soul that isn't willing to be confined by what others say is true, the soul who is willing to find her own way, discovering strength and character, insight, intuition and courage, and who is willing to pursue her dream despite the odds.

What We Know or Don't

Copernicus said, *"To know that we know what we know, and to know that we do not know what we do not know; that is true knowledge."*

A protégé is someone who doesn't know how to get himself to the next level in his journey of success. Sometimes he's so entrenched in the details that he lacks perspective. Often he doesn't know what he doesn't know.

TIP   **WHO OWNS YOUR LIFE**

Whose fault is it?

"If only the circumstances were different, I could make progress. If only someone else would change their approach, if only the economy would improve, if only, if only."

One of the great lessons I was taught as a child is: you may not control what happens to you but you do control how you respond.

You and your protégé live in the real world. Admit it. And take control of your life. Spend your energies working on what you can do, not the reasons why you can't.

That sounds like double talk, but let's think about this. You know what you know – that's what you've learned up until now, the experiences you've had that guide your beliefs and your choices.

And you know what you don't know – all those things in the world that aren't within your ken. Perhaps it's thermonuclear physics. Perhaps it's starting a fire without a match. Perhaps it's staying upright on a surfboard. For me, it's all that and more! There's so much that I know I don't know.

My blind spot lies in the area where I don't know what I don't know. It makes sense that if I were to find my knowledge deficient in a specific area, I could potentially gather enough knowledge and practical experience to acquire a skill. I could make my wife extremely happy if I took a cooking course and learned my way around the kitchen. I know for sure that I don't know, and I know how and where I could learn. I'm just lacking the impetus to do so, in spite of my wife's urging. I know what I don't know in that area.

But I don't know what I don't know that, if I knew it, could change my relationship with my wife. And sometimes it takes a good friend to point it out to me. "You mean that if I just shut up and listen instead of trying to fix things for her, she'd be happier with me?" How come I couldn't figure that out myself? Because I didn't know what I didn't know – that she is just looking for someone to vent to, to get it off her chest, to feel heard. She knows perfectly well what to do about her problem; she doesn't need me to tell her. She just needs me to listen, to be a sounding board, to care. Whoa!

A mentor's task is to be that guiding light – to get to know your protégé well enough to see what he doesn't see, and to shine a light on that so he can learn, grow and move to the next level.

Self Talk

Some describe intimacy this way: "in-to-me-see". A mentor and her protégé become intimate. They see into each other – they see more than the parts that make up the whole. They see the synergy that the whole creates.

How does that intimacy happen? Through conversation. All connection occurs through conversation. In any interaction between two people, there are several conversations that occur.

There's the conversation that consists of what you say to me and what I say to you. That's the external conversation.

Then there's the conversation you have about what I'm saying. "I wonder why he's saying that. What does he really mean? Does he think that I think that way? I'm not sure I agree."

Then there's the conversation you have about me. "I wonder

where he learned all of this. Does he really know what he's talking about? I'm sure he does – I've seen his work and I know he's capable."

Then there's the conversation you have about yourself. "What am I doing here? Is this what I really want? Do I think I can pull this off? I must be nuts to think I can do it. Still, he sounds like he believes in me. Why not try?"

Then there's the whole conversation you have about the world you live in, driven by your belief systems, by society, by upbringing, by experiences...it's like the water a fish swims in. Does the fish really know it's in water?

Most of these conversations go on inside of us unchecked – in fact, unrecognized. We don't realize we're having these conversations, yet each of them has a strong and important influence on us. The conversations are often about what we don't know we don't know.

The mentor's job is to help identify those conversations – what is it the protégé is telling herself that holds her back? Moves her forward? Which conversations serve and which constrain? And the mentor helps the protégé to manage those conversations – to choose which ones to listen to and which ones deserve the mute button.

And don't forget to check in with which conversation is going on. It's funny, but sometimes my protégé doesn't hear what I've said. I don't mean that she's not listening; I mean that she's listening   to something else. People hear what they want to hear. People often hear what they need to hear. Sometimes what I say leads my protégé to a whole new train of thought – which may actually be where she needs to go. But watch out!! You may not be aware that she's gone there, and your connection gets broken. So check in.

When someone hears something I didn't say it is pivotal for her to realize that she's hearing her own conversation – she's talking to herself. She must identify the difference between what I've said and what she heard. As her mentor, I want to know what she's telling herself so I can be a check and balance. I want to imprint that conversation if it's great, and if what I did want to say still wants to be heard then I say it. But if the lights went on and the conversation changed, let's spend some time in that bright light, discovering its meaning for her now.

Portrait of a Mentor

This question reminds me of the first line of Elizabeth Barrett Browning's poem: *"How do I love thee? Let me count the ways"*

Mentoring is a way of being, so the characteristics of a mentor are described in being: being empathetic, showing concern, being genuine, being authentic, being curious, asking questions, listening, showing self-control, being a catalyst, being a resource.

Just as important is what a mentor isn't: a cheerleader. A wizard. A caretaker. A comic. A rescuer. Mentoring is about drawing out the best in someone else - not doing it for them.

The primary modus operandi, the MO, of the mentor is humility, caring and an uncompromising desire for the protégé to become fully what he is made to become. As mentor, I want to be the nutrient, the catalyst for greatness.

Being Known

What people long for is to be known. That's what this is about. Someone is prepared to let you know them, and you are prepared to be known yourself. Then you begin your walk through the conversation. Your protégé wants you to truly "get" what she is all about. To then create momentum, movement forward, propulsion, direction. To launch her over obstacles. To build a foundation upon which she can stand. She wants to know you've got her back. You're right behind her, beside her, supporting, guiding, coaching, urging.

Isaac Newton said it best: *"If I have been able to see further, it was only because I stood on the shoulders of giants."*

Dear Journal:

Today I spent time with Andy just talking and getting to know one another. If I'm going to mentor him, he'll have to trust me.

I guess the mere fact that he asked for my help is a sign of trust, but I can't help thinking that it goes further than that. Andy is giving me a huge responsibility in allowing me to advise him. I need to honor that trust.

And I need to get to know Andy intimately - what drives him, what he's afraid of. Boy, he really responded to my favorite question: "What is it that you don't want to tell me?" He was open, honest and humble - all qualities of a great leader.

I am humbled just to be with him, and I must treat his confidences with great respect. He has been through a lot of hardship and weathered it well to get where he is. I mustn't forget that as I urge him to risk. And he has to know that what happens between us stays between us - I will not break his confidence.

And no matter what, Andy needs to feel that I'm not only listening to him speak, but also that I'm hearing what he's saying. I shake my head when I think of some of the conversations I've had. Some people only hear what they want to hear. And some, instead of listening to me, are preparing for what they want to say next. I won't dishonor Andy in that way.

I'm eagerly anticipating our next meeting - this is going to be a great journey!

Chapter 2

The Mentor as Confidante
"Can I Trust You, Really Trust You?'

"Can I trust you?" Those words echo in my head each and every time I enter into a mentoring relationship. The mentor/protégé relationship is so precious, so fragile. What a treasure it is to be trusted, and what a monumental responsibility it is to take on that trust!

This vibrant, energetic person with great talent and huge   potential is asking you to guide his passage through a minefield, and trusts that you will be accurate every step of the way. Not only does he trust you to give him precise information, he expects you to be kind, compassionate and forgiving when he ignores your advice and takes a few steps in the other direction!

Your task is to create the kind of environment where she trusts you completely, takes your advice without question, follows you blindly in faith where there is no proof. Wow! This is a humbling experience, and your success as a mentor will depend on your   ability to be humble.

Jim Collins, in his book _Good to Great_, describes the most effective leader as having fierce resolve combined with great humility; giving credit to others when things go well and taking responsibility in times of struggle. A great mentor is someone who is willing to forget herself; who is focused wholly on the protégé and who is willing to set aside her own struggles and successes for the sake of learning alongside the learner.

Being humble means suspending judgment about the person who has said he is willing to trust your advice. And in being humble, creating trust, developing a faith-filled relationship, you create the clearing for your follower to see you as his confidante. Confidante – a trusted friend, advisor, one with whom to unburden his heart, to be open, honest, trusting. It takes courage to assign another individual the role of Confidante – treat that commitment gently, with honor and respect, for it is not made lightly.

A humble Confidante is without judgment for the person who has said he is willing to trust your advice.

A humble Confidante is supportive and accepting of the individual even when her actions are misguided, inappropriate, or just plain wrong.

A humble Confidante is fully trustworthy, maintaining the confidentiality of the relationship as fiercely as if it were in confession.

A humble Confidante is clear with the protégé, without having to be right. There is no "I told you so!" in a mentoring relationship.

A humble Confidante asks questions not for her own understanding, but so that the protégé understands.

A humble Confidante is at peace with the place the protégé is at, quiet, calm, just being together without feeling the need to intervene.

A humble Confidante allows the protégé to speak without allowing an internal conversation to drown out what is being said.

A humble Confidante stirs the emotions of the protégé like the coals of a fire; causing the flame of passion to flare each time it seems that setbacks or discouragement may quench it.

A humble Confidante is in the moment, not needing to look good, be right, be in control or be comfortable.

A humble Confidante is aware that there is only one person's agenda in this relationship.

A humble Confidante loves the protégé where he is, but sees where he can be, calling to him from that place.

A humble Confidante is patient while the protégé finds her way by following the sound of the mentoring voice.

A humble Confidante hears what's really being said, not what he wants to hear, nor what he thinks he hears.

A humble Confidante admits his own mistakes, his own fears, his own doubts and insecurities when this will encourage the protégé to face her own.

A humble Confidante has a servant's heart – the greatest leaders are those who serve. By so doing, the mentor will gain in return the trust and loyalty of the protégé, and will have sown in her   the seeds of greatness that others will see as humility and servanthood.

Are you thinking to yourself, "I didn't get where I am by being humble?" I think, maybe you did! Don't confuse being humble with being spineless. That's why Collins talks about fierce resolve – determination and strength and focus and a willingness to fight for that which you believe - these are the characteristics of a great leader and a great mentor. On this foundation of resolve you stand while lifting up your protégé to stand as well.

Are you asking yourself now, how do I build this humble relationship?

The answer to that question is: listening and hearing.

Generous Listening

Every mentor first and foremost is a Confidante - a person who listens without judgment, who hears his protégé fully, openly and honestly. The most important skill a mentor has is the ability to listen attentively.

The first task in listening attentively is to create the environment for open, honest and frank communication to take place. Real exploration takes trust. Trust is created in a place of comfort and safety, a place where the protégé is not afraid of being hurt, a place where it is safe to risk, and where self-examination and self-discovery are both anticipated and expected. This role may take a while to solidify – it takes patience and intention to develop trust.

Sharing life, sharing stories, demands personal, face-to-face interaction. So much of our communication is entwined not in what is being said, but what is heard through tone of voice and physical communication. It is commonly known that only 7% of what is being said is actually in the words we choose. 38% of our communication is in the tone of voice that we use, and the remainder, 55% lies in the body language we project while we speak. To communicate only by telephone eliminates a significant amount of the information we send and receive. The written word says almost nothing yet opens up a whole minefield of opportunities to misinterpret. Our own internal conversation fills in the parts that are blank, and we are often less than accurate!

So I recommend that you mentor one-to-one, face-to-face. That way, you are totally "in it" with the protégé. For the moment, he is the most important person you know and listening to him is the most important thing you can do. You can receive the full message, and you can see and hear what's behind those carefully chosen words. Don't forget, the protégé will initially want to look good, feel comfortable, be right and be in control, so he will put his best foot forward, enrolling you in his worthiness to be mentored. And he is worthy! The mere fact that he has requested your assistance means that he recognizes the need to learn and grow to his fullest potential, and that he will be better equipped to climb that mountain with a guide.

However, as you hear his story, there will be more and more opportunity for the real human being to appear: the one with flat spots that need to be shaped, fears to be assuaged, demons to be wrestled and uncertainties to be swept out of the way. And much of the real protégé shows up in his presence – the one you see in his body and hear in his voice, the one that can't hide behind the written word and the anonymity of the telephone.

Keep your ears tuned to hear words that express emotion. This is critical! Words like frustrated, afraid, excited, scared, bored, disappointed, tired, on-fire – they all indicate significance in your protégé's life. When you hear an emotion word like one of these, let her finish her sentence, then ask about the emotion.

"Tell me about bored." "What does on fire look like?" This is your check-in, and your ability to hear the words and direct the conversation is the foundation of the relationship. Philosopher Martin Heidegger said, "Language is the house of being." Every word is significant.

TIP	FEELINGS...NOTHING MORE THAN FEELINGS

Facts are interesting. Data is valuable. Information can be important. But growth rises and falls at the level of emotion. Emotion causes the protégé to remember skills and information; she grows as she gains confidence in applying what she is learning.

I can never emphasize enough how critical the skill of listening is for the mentor. The higher plane of listening is discernment – what are you listening for?

Be extra sensitive to hear every emotion-based word your protégé says. Hard-edged words like frustration, fear, anger, exhaustion, etc. are the keys to who he are and who you can help him become. Similarly, listen for the positive emotion words: excitement, pride, thrill, contented, warm. These feelings are ones that you will hope to recreate in them often by reminding them in the attendant situation.

This is very important. In fact, so important that individual emotion words are the one thing I will write down during the conversation.

They are too important to forget. (I don't like to take notes during the conversation; it's distracting and it assaults the sense of presence that I have worked to build.)

Don't leave an emotion word unpacked. Say things like: "A moment ago you used the word 'frustration'; tell me about that." Or, "Enthused is such a great word; what makes you chose that particular word?"

And ensure they answer your question. "I still don't see the resentment' you speak of; help me understand it."

Much of your task in listening to your protégé lies in your "way of being" – and you can facilitate that through a series of non-verbal listening techniques. In the beginning, you may feel as though this is contrived; continuous practice will cause you to assimilate these techniques so that over time, they become a natural part of your interactions with anyone and everyone.

By now you're saying, okay, get on with the doing part! So here's the "doing" of the "being":

- Be fully present – so often we think that we are paying attention when really our mind is wandering somewhere far, far away – to do lists, the last conversation we were involved in, what's coming up on the weekend – even something as simple as what we're going to say when the person we're engaged with stops talking! So often our own internal conversation is louder than the one we're in – what we think about what she's thinking! Stay focused. Keep an open, curious mind. Stay conscious of your surroundings and the individual. Come from a genuine desire to learn, grow, and understand through your interaction with the other. Don't just act interested, BE interested!

- Keep your mouth closed. Does that sound a little strong? It's meant to! It's difficult not to interrupt with a question or an opinion, and I beg you to resist. I have a consultant friend who meets his clients over lunch – that way he can put food in his mouth to prevent himself from talking too much!

- Be aware of yourself physically. Be sure to stay on the same physical level as your client – no power plays here! This person trusts you, and you trust her – there's no need to create any form of advantage. Physically being at the same level gives you the opportunity to make clear, open eye contact, to acknowledge through facial expressions and gestures that you understand what is being said, and creates the space for you to lean forward with interest.

- In an early life as a radio reporter I was given a very interesting image that works so well in conversation.

Imagine there is a microphone in your hand. Imagine holding it in front of your protégé when you ask your question. When he finishes answering, look him directly in the eye and push the microphone two inches closer to his mouth – figuratively speaking, of course! He will speak again, and what is said will be even more revealing than what was said in the first place. Keep the image of the microphone in your mind throughout the discussion and you will get closer to the truth.

- Be aware of your own filters. We all listen through our own filters; what we want to hear, what we expect to hear, what we think we hear. Anticipating what will be said closes possibilities for further exploration. Indeed, the speaker will intuit that you have made an assessment or a judgment – you won't be able to keep it off your face! So be conscious of staying away from your bias (your opinion of the speaker, of what she is saying, of the way you think things *should* look), positive or negative, and also beware of any cultural myths or assumptions that may have hold of you.

- Be aware also of your own emotional triggers – both positive and negative. We all are susceptible to emotional reactions to thought, word, and deed. Having high emotional intelligence implies that you are able to man age your own emotions and the emotional response you experience with others. There are going to be some things that you have strong opinions about – individuals, events, language. Notice how you respond when your client becomes defensive or aggressive. Practice staying neutral. Watch for buzzwords that are used to deflect honesty or responsibility and challenge them in a non-emotional, neutral way. Avoid using profanities or expletives – it's never wrong to take the high road with language.

- Finally, when and if you check out – you lose your focus, your attention wanders, you get distracted or you realize you've just missed out on the last minute or two of conversation – admit it! Acknowledge that you had a brain cramp, ask forgiveness, go back to the last item you clearly remember and go again. The atmosphere changes when listening stops, and the speaker will notice, so don't try to fool him. It's disrespectful, and you might have missed something important. Be humble and go again.

Listening Prompts

I can hear you right now – "So what about the way *I* verbally interact? After all, doesn't a conversation go both ways? And isn't this person here to get *my* advice? When do *I* get to say something? I'm about bursting at the seams with wisdom!" Some very effective uses of words to enhance listening:

- Begin with a question – then let your client talk…and talk…and talk… In fact, let her talk until she's finished – use your facial expressions and the occasional "uh-huh" and "carry on" until she winds down. Often people who are talking find their way to a solution just listening to themselves.
- When she's finished, replay the essence of what you heard with NO additions. You could say, "What I'm hearing you say is…did I get it right?" Then listen to her response – you need to check in to make sure you did get it right, and she needs to be able to correct or regroup. You both need to be on the same page and not relying on each other's translation or interpretation.
- Paraphrase what was said in your own words – this gives her a chance to verify your understanding, and to hear it expressed differently. Be brief and neutral – neither approving nor disapproving.
- A very strong approach is to ascribe a feeling to what was just said – this gives her a chance to adjust if you're not on target. When you get it wrong, she will correct

you because no one likes to have people confused about what she's feeling. When you get it right, she will expand on it.

- Ask her to repeat what was said in a different way. You could say things like, "Come at me again with that; I don't want to miss anything." Or, "Back up for a second, I want to get my head around what you're saying."

- Ask open-ended questions that require a thoughtful response, more than just yes or no. One common mistake listeners make is to ask leading questions, and then answer those questions themselves. And those leading questions often have judgment in them, which will definitely close down possibilities! Good questions: "What's behind that?" "How's that working for you?" and "What were you thinking?" (NOT *What were you thinking?!*)

- Ask for examples to illustrate what's being said – you get more from a story than from instruction. An example can give you context as well as content, and you'll have a clearer picture of the situation.

- Describe what you see in her behavior – be specific about the observable actions. Do not attribute motives to her behavior, and don't make assessments about her personality or character traits based on your observations. She's perfectly capable of doing that all by herself. A mentor's role is to create possibility for growth and change in a generous way.

- And remember, the word "but" negates everything that you've just said. It says "I didn't really mean what I said first, I just put it in there to be nice." A "but" is a sugar coated "no". Be assertive and positive in a generous way.

You know you're finished listening and have an opening for movement into offering information when they ask. Listen for, "So what do you think?" "So what should I do?" "Can you help me?" "What's your advice?" What sweet words for a mentor to hear – the protégé is becoming coachable. Watch for a smile – that's your invitation to speak into her life. And if you don't hear those questions, it's time to ask, "And how can I help?"

You are the **Confidante**. It feels safe to be around you. People want to talk to you; they tell you their story. They open up you. They risk. What a marvellous legacy to leave: "People trusted you." Perhaps that legacy might have a second line: "people listened to you."

Dear Journal:

My first mentoring session with Andy went well. In my role as mentor, I'm getting to know him in a whole new way. I didn't realize how much he knew about his industry. Very impressive!

Like so many others, he's so close to the business of doing business that he doesn't see the pattern he's developing. What's the expression - you can't see the forest for the trees?

He's so busy doing the doing that he's lost perspective about the whole picture.

So that's my role as Andy's mentor, I guess. I have to help him identify what's important - values, passion, style. Who is Andy? And what's he up to? That is, where does he think he's going in life, and is that where he wants to go?

The toughest part today was keeping my opinions to myself. I have to remember that it's not all about me! What I think Andy should do is irrelevant, really. My job is to pull out of Andy what it is he's trying to become.

The best part is - he listens to every word I say as if it were gospel! If only I could get my own children to do the same!!!

Chapter Three

The Mentor as Sage "Wisdom: Seeing Fifteen Minutes into the Future"

It's very likely that you're reading this book because someone has asked you to help, to provide advice, to lead him along the path to success. And the reason he has made that request is because he thinks you know what to do! "I know what to do?" I don't see myself that way at all. I just fumble my way along, make mistakes and fix them, and learn not to make the same mistake again.

That may or may not be true for you. However, what is true is that somehow you've made it seem easy or at least doable. The person making this request respects you for your skills and abilities, for your way of being, for your past performance, evidence that you know what to do and how to do it.

In fact, he thinks you're a sage, the Sage, the wise one – of all the people he could have asked, you topped the list. What an honor! And you need to treat this request with the honor and respect it deserves. We often find it difficult to receive praise and accolades, but receive we should, recognizing the awesome responsibilities that accompany this kind of request.

What is a sage? The Encarta Dictionary defines a sage as: *somebody who is regarded as knowledgeable, wise, and experienced, especially a person of advanced years revered for his wisdom and good judgment.* It's that influence and respect that drew your protégé to choose you. And by choosing you, he charged you with the task of duplicating yourself in a different mold with different raw materials. Sound intimidating? It doesn't need to be. It requires you to be able to reflect on what and who you are and how you came to be this way, and then to recount those experiences to your protégé in a way to which he can relate.

As Sage, you need to get a feel for the protégé's future, and to coach her in visualizing, identifying and understanding her own long-term objective. What are her values, mission, capabilities and style? So many of these are internal; you have to mine the depths to discover them. The protégé is giving you mineral rights, and is working the mine with you. Once they're uncovered, as a team you embrace them and keep them in front of you. (I am indebted to Susan Scott for the mineral rights idea. Please read her great book **Fierce Conversations**.)

There's a parallel shaft to the mine – that shaft mines the protégé's vision where his goals, strategies and tactics are embedded. You, as the Sage, know how to ensure that there is a growth objective and plan in place that reflects the protégé's sense of purpose.

The Sage role has two parts – the first is to help the protégé identify and understand his values, vision and goals. The second, which we'll discuss in a later chapter, relates to keeping these values, vision, goals and the progress toward them in front of the protégé on an ongoing basis to maintain focus.

As Sage, you help the protégé with self-reflection. You are to encourage him to understand who he is, what he's made of and what he's made for. Awareness of self helps the protégé to know that every action he undertake either draws him closer to his destiny or moves him further away.

I'm always surprised when I begin this discussion at how little people really know about themselves. Questions like "Who are you?" "What are you good at that no one else does better?" "What does success look like?" "What's the one talent you're known for?" often draw blank stares and stuttering. I always wonder how we can get so far in our careers without being aware of who we are and what we can do.

Self-awareness is so key to success in whatever endeavors your protégé is pursuing. Searching out what we don't know about ourselves, discovering daily the things that drive us, the things that hold us back – this exercise is an essential part of the daily work of transformation – reinventing ourselves to be the person we want to be, and the one who will have the success we want to have.

C2 Matrix: Confidence/Competence

I've mapped out a matrix that shows the relationship between the internal person and the external objectives – the raw material and what we want to do with it. The two parts, internal and external, have to be in alignment for success to ensue. Any misalignment will derail the protégé's progress, and it's your role, as the mentor to make sure that doesn't happen. Derailments are messy and take a long time to clean up!

It wouldn't hurt for you as the mentor, to think through this process yourself prior to leading someone else through it!

C2 Matrix: Confidence/Competence

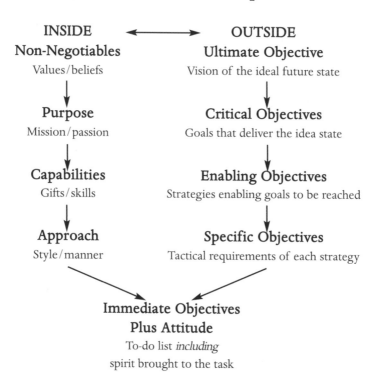

INSIDE ◄————► OUTSIDE

Non-Negotiables   **Ultimate Objective**
Values/beliefs   Vision of the ideal future state

Purpose   **Critical Objectives**
Mission/passion   Goals that deliver the idea state

Capabilities   **Enabling Objectives**
Gifts/skills   Strategies enabling goals to be reached

Approach   **Specific Objectives**
Style/manner   Tactical requirements of each strategy

Immediate Objectives
Plus Attitude
To-do list *including*
spirit brought to the task

The left hand column, headed INSIDE, answers the question, "Who are you?" In it, you discover the protégé's values, mission, gifts and style – all the things that make her uniquely her. This is the hardware side of the operation.

The right hand column, headed OUTSIDE, focuses on where she wants to go. The first objective – the ultimate objective – asks, "Who are you becoming?" The next three objectives – critical, enabling and specific objectives, answer the question "What are you going to do to get there?" And the final coming together at the bottom of the matrix answers "What does this mean for you *today*? What will you do?" This is the software side of the operation. The hardware side is the equipment we've got to work with. The software side is how we program it to work to its optimum potential.

Every time you and your protégé meet, the mentoring conversations will touch each of the nine components of the matrix. Be clear about each area before you move to an action plan. Some days it will be easy to know which component is important. Other days you, as the Sage, will have to choose a starting point and build from there. The conversation you have will lead you to the right conclusion – just be open to beginning with the end in mind.

The Inside

While the temptation is often to talk about what the protégé is going to *do*, a real mentor is working on who the protégé *is* and what he is destined to *become*. That sounds like heady stuff, but it's critical. He must discover and define who he is. That will give confidence in his value and worth. I am sometimes amazed by the shift in someone's capacity to succeed and in his immediate intentions just by exploring his strengths and abilities. When he gives himself permission to be himself, his growth is phenomenal. I imagine this to be like the moth coming out of the chrysalis – the struggle to identify self creates the strength needed to fly.

Non-Negotiables
We all have things on which we absolutely will not

compromise. These are our deepest values and beliefs. They arise from inside, they form the foundation of a person's life, who they are, and who they desire to become. These cannot be taken lightly. They must be uncovered, named, and understood. Our core beliefs come from a lifetime of experience – from our upbringing, our family values, our peers at school and at work, our successes and failures, the people we have and do admire, societal norms and beliefs, generational values.

Usually they are fixed and firm. Once we're convinced about something, it's tough to change our opinions. You, as the mentor, need to watch that you do NOT try to impose your own non-negotiables on the protégé. This will be a huge temptation, especially since you know what worked for you! Understand that what worked for you did so because of your values and beliefs, and what worked for you may not be the same for your protégé. You have to lead her to discover her own, and to decide where that will lead her in her quest for success. Remember, you're not recreating your own success. You're facilitating a new success, uniquely belonging to your protégé, with your fingerprints only lightly on it, if at all.

You must help her to identify what is not negotiable and affirm that this is who she is and that the fullest expression of her life is in these values. You may find, in this process, that the experiences that created these values were less than excellent for your protégé. You may find that some of her values conflict with each other, and part of your role as the Sage is to coach your protégé about which of the conflicting values will serve her in achieving her goal. You will coach her on how to live and manage the conflict she might experience in the process. For example, a strong sense of responsibility to family can cause conflict when the path chosen to succeed involves long hours and travel away from home. Offering advice and resources and assisting in the problem solving process, can help her to keep those conflicting values in alignment. If the potential for conflict is not identified, it can blindside your protégé at a time when she really needs to be focused. Thus, awareness of self is critical to the success of the matrix, and to the future of your protégé. She's depending on you to guide her through these shark-infested waters!

Discovering the non-negotiables can be done in an infinite number of ways, and I have a couple of favorites. First, I like to tell a lot of stories and anecdotes about how things work for me, and as I do this, I listen closely to my protégé's responses. Does he identify with these stories? Does he look at me with that RCA Victor dog kind of look? Does he ask me how I can possibly function this way, or does he say, "Yeah, I do that too, how can I change that to work better?"

And I listen to the stories he has to tell me – in fact much of what I want to get from him lives in the stories and examples he gives me. I can learn more about him from the way he describes his interactions with other people that I can when he summarizes his skills and talents. Why? Because his behavior shows who he really is. Ralph Waldo Emerson once said, "What you do speaks so loudly that what you say I can't hear." A person will often describe who he wants to be rather than who he is, but who he is rings loud and clear in what he does. So I really want my protégé to tell me some stories.

Another technique I like to use is to ask my protégé to make a   list of 100 things she would like to do before she dies. Try this yourself. I find the first 25 – 30 items are fairly easy to come up with. After that, the list becomes a struggle – up to #75 or so. Then it gets easy; in fact it's hard to stop. And, most importantly, the items at the bottom of the list are the most valuable. These are the things that live in the soul. The really meaningful things. The ones that come after all the materialistic and ego goals are met. These are the things that matter.

I assign this task to my protégé, but I rarely read the list. I ask her, "What do you notice about the list? What do you see?" The conclusions she draws here assist her in coming up with the things that are the most important in her life – her non-negotiables.

Purpose

This is what he is here for. What is his mission? What is his passion? What makes his heart sing? What pulls him to do more and work hard? What gets him out of bed in the morning? What does he really want to have happen in his life and the world around him? What does he want his children to say about him?

This is what drives him. Many people haven't really thought about this, but when they do, life explodes with opportunity and with a sense of drive that is exciting and fulfilling.

Sometimes in this discussion, I go to the question, "What would you do if time and money were no object?" I have him imagine what they would do if he could do only those things he likes to do, and then we work on how to make that happen. Sometimes, I ask him how long he expects to live, and then ask what he's going to do between now and then that could match the progress he's made over the equivalent number of years from now back. Most of us expect to live to 70 or 80 years of age, and most of the people being coached are between 35 and 50 – imagine what another 20 or 30 years of productivity could look like? Especially knowing what we know and having what we have. Wow! What a contribution each of us could be!

This is the purpose discussion. Many people at the mentoring stage are asking themselves, in the immortal words of the song, "Is That All There Is?" Have you known anyone on the employment ladder who was totally focused on the next rung of the ladder, always the next one and the next one? The mentoring process is so valuable in being clear about where your protégé wants to go, and making sure his ladder is propped up on the right wall.

Capabilities

Capabilities are an inventory of the gifts, skills and talents that your protégé has been given and developed. Understanding who you are and what you can do is important. Equally important is to understand who you aren't and what you can't do. Some of the things we don't do well can be improved with training and skill – some of these things are innate and can't be changed. Even if we decide to train ourselves up for a skill or task, we have to have a baseline capacity for that particular capability.

Each of us is created perfect, whole and completely equipped for the tasks we are given to do (our purpose). Sometimes I hear people struggle with improving their weaknesses and I want to shake them and whoever told them to do that! None of us is good at everything. If we were, what a boring world this would be! We need to be adequate at all the tasks we are expected to complete. I can do laundry and fold, but I do it badly. Fortunately, my wife is more domestically inclined. Now, I really value her skills, talents and desire in that area, and I appreciate that she takes care of the things that I do badly!

I don't want to trivialize the issue. I do want to stress that this matrix is about your protégé and the things he can do exceptionally well. And sometimes, that's difficult to identify. It's not that difficult to identify the things we do poorly – somehow they seem to stand out! We can find people who do those things well, find a way to connect with them and leverage our skills together.

There are a variety of ways to discover our skills, gifts and talents. You may be aware of some assessments that you find particularly helpful. At the back of this book, you can find a variety of assessments that I am aware of and find useful. This list is by no means exhaustive, and many others are available for your use in assisting your protégé to self discover his strengths.

The more information your protégé can gather that will give him insight into the facets of his performance profile, the more accurate he can be about his self assessment, and the more confident he will be about his ability to achieve, with your guidance, the objectives and goals he sets for himself.

Approach

Everyone has a unique style as to how they work and how they get things done. Each of us deals with different people in different ways. Your protégé must be able to analyze and understand her own style in dealing with people and to assess its success.

It is also critically important that both you and your protégé understand the manner you use to work and deal with people. Your style must be workable and acceptable to your protégé. Of course, it's safe to assume that your style matches his, since he has selected you to be his mentor. Still, you and he need to be clear and up front about what each of you can expect in terms of the style you use to interact together to ensure an effective coaching environment.

TIP   **WHO DO YOU THINK YOU ARE ANYWAY?**

If you are interested in some assessments that can increase your self-awareness, I would recommend you use some form of personality assessment such as the MBTI (Myers-Briggs Type Indicator) or DISC system. The Kolbe Conative Instinct assessment evaluates an individual's striving instinct in accomplishing tasks. The Strengthsfinder profile from Gallup determines which five of 34 strengths dominate the way we interact with task and people. Some form of 360 feedback tool provides invaluable information about the impact we have on others and their interpretation of our performance. And the Leadership Practices Inventory by Kouzes and Posner give good insight into our grasp of leadership qualities and their application. Remember, though, that assessments are a good idea, but are not required for accurate self-awareness. Some people use them as a form of confirmation of what they already instinctively know.

The Outside

Most people understand that they need a plan. Many know how to plan. Few actually do it! You've heard the expression that people who fail to plan – plan to fail! I really think that failure to plan, to think ahead, is often a result of inertia – when you're working and living and trying to juggle a whole lot of demands, days turn into weeks, turn into months, turn into years, and when you turn around, life is passing by without notice. A well thought out, documented plan can prevent that from happening, and can keep your protégé focused on the goals he wants to achieve and the dreams he wants to accomplish.

What follows here is a step-by-step process that leads to specific actions performed right now that will move the protégé down the path to those dreams. Each of these steps should be considered in sequence for greatest effect. Any proposed actions should be evaluated with respect to their contribution to the next link in the chain.

| TIP | WHAT COLOUR IS THE SKY IN YOUR WORLD? |

People love to talk in concepts. They enjoy musing about where they are and what they might do. They like to see problems, issues that are in the way; they like to talk about the reasons they can't do something rather than the actions needed to move forward.

It is important to keep the protégé grounded in the real world. Do that by asking regularly about the specific impact a particular circumstance is having on them right now. Challenge their impact answers. Ask again. Push them. Help them to see reality in all its glory and all its starkness.

Then, move their eyes to the future. Ask implication questions. What will your world look like in six months if this doesn't change? With no strategy to deal with this, what will you be facing this time next year? Will you feel any different at that time?

Impact and implication questions are a key tool in your toolbox. They keep the conversation real. They move from excuses to the kind of reality that delivers action.

Ultimate Objective

What is the protégé's long-term vision for his life? This differs from mission in that mission is a sense of calling, and vision is the sense of destiny. If your protégé could accomplish something great, what would it be?

I like to ask my protégé to pick a date in the future – two years, five years, twenty years from today – and ask him to tell me what his life looks like. "What do you spend your day doing? Who do you talk to? Where do you do your work? What does your home look like? Your family? What's on display in your office or on your walls at home that is significant?" I have him give me the answers to these questions in the present tense, as if it is already so. This is a form of self-talk. The subconscious mind cannot distinguish between what is real and what is vividly imagined. The brain registers the information it hears as if it were so, and creates an imagined picture. The thinker is then drawn back to that image over and over again. The more you see it, the more you think it's possible to accomplish. So the answers to these questions describing his life become essential to his success.

Critical Objectives

How will your protégé reach the ideal state – by setting goals or critical objectives? These goals can be short term and long term. Both are important. Your protégé may have some things she wants to accomplish in short order – within a month or two. There are others that may take a few years. The more goals that are set and met, the greater the sense of accomplishment, and the greater the chance of pursuing the process to completion. More importantly, measurement of these goals will tell your protégé what steps she has achieved that lead her to her highest calling. And, of course, these goals must be SMART – Specific, Measurable, Attainable, Realistic, and Time Related. (More about this later.)

Enabling Objectives

What are the strategies that the person will use to reach their goals? Here the real planning is done to help the person identify what they need to do. This is the "how" of goal setting. At this point, your protégé may have set some goals he thinks is impossible. In fact, I recommend that he does. George Bernard Shaw once said that all progress depends on the unreasonable man. That struck me as essential to the mentoring process. If your protégé isn't stretching himself to achieve what he wants to achieve, what is he really at stake for? So strive for the impossible. Ask yourself, if it were possible, how could I do it? There are a million different ways to get the job done. The strategy to accomplish the goal may change, even though the goal itself is not likely to change.

We might visit this step more than once as we try and fail. I like to think of failure as "failing magnificently". Even if we miss the mark, we've accomplished some of what we set out to, and we've learned a great deal along the way – especially how not to do it next time! So I see failure as a form of victory, and the best part is…we get to go again!

Specific Objectives

In being specific, we can create tactics and options that will serve us in achieving the objective. Breaking each strategy down into bite-sized pieces will get your protégé to his goal. Choosing what to do and when to do it is critical for achieving success. The more specific your protégé is about his intent, the greater his chance of success. And with being specific comes the opportunity to make promises (commitments to get the job done) and requests (for assistance from other people). Many of the goals we set we mistakenly think we can accomplish on our own without help of any kind. "If it's to be, it's up to me." That's a lot of pressure to put on oneself, when there are any number of people surrounding your protégé who are willing to participate in mutual success. The Bible says, "You do not have because you do not ask." And that is so often true in our day-to-day activities. So be specific, be focused and be clear about asking for help.

Immediate Objectives **plus** Attitude

Tying together the inside (hardware) and the outside (software) to make the program run is that special combination of task and desire. A skill without drive is wasted talent. Drive without skills is fruitless striving. Together they are an unbeatable combination.

Your role as a mentor is to make sure that these two paths are aligned so that the effort your protégé is making will bear fruit.

Fully completing a few specific things and having a well-chosen attitude/approach will create unprecedented progress. And of the two, attitude is really the greater effort, and has the greater effect. Your protégé can choose to see all the things that aren't working. He can give you a list of all the things that have gone wrong, all the reasons why this idea won't work, all the problems he faces in accomplishing this task. Or he can see the problems he faces as challenges to be overcome. Framing is key. Is the glass half empty or half full? If it can't be done this way, how *can* it be done? If it didn't work, did he learn something and change his ways? Is he going to quit?

What she is going to do today and the attitude she is going to bring to the effort will make everything real, immediate and do-able. This step is about keeping focused on the goal, using all the skills and abilities given to her and learned by her, and following a goal-setting plan that can lead her to accomplishment. This step is about knowing the world and being true to who she is.

Guiding the Conversation

This role as a Sage is the overarching role in mentoring. Each of these components in the *C2 Matrix: Confidence/Competence* must be considered in each mentoring conversation, perhaps consciously, always unconsciously. Different components will take on different significance depending on the progress of your protégé. And you as a mentor will wear a different hat, or a different role, depending on what's wanted and needed as the two of you journey together. You may decide to give your protégé a copy of the tool we've drawn out in this chapter – some people learn better by looking at a model. For others, it will confuse, so you might just lead them through it one step at a time. Choose wisely. After all, you are the Sage! Your mission is to help your protégé uncover who he will be at his best, and to help them accelerate that becoming.

You are the **Sage**. You share in your protégé's deepest dreams, hopes, aspirations and possibilities. You voyage together with individuals who do amazing things, reach exciting goals and make a genuine difference. You have the wisdom of the **Sage**; let your wisdom flow.

Dear Journal:

I asked Andy why he chose me to be his mentor and I was surprised at his answer.

I've known Andy since he first started working with our organization after graduation. I trained him as a "newby" - showed him the ropes until he got his feet on the ground. He was a quick learner then, and still is. I've kept my eye on him as he's made his way through different levels of responsibility. He shows great leadership, as well as common sense. Why would he need my help?

Andy told me that he's trusted me from the first day we met. He appreciated my taking him under my wing, and any time he had a tough decision to make, he always asked himself what I would do. Whatever the answer, that's what he'd do. And since he'd always been successful using that tactic, it only made sense to formalize the relationship by asking me to mentor him at this critical time in his career.

Who knew? I just did what I'd want someone to do for me, knowing he would be lost without someone to ask. I didn't realize that he looked upon me as a role model - wow! I'd better be careful about what I do. I'd hate for someone to start duplicating the activities that I'd call less than excellent!

It's humbling. You never know the impact you have on someone else until they tell you!

Chapter Four

The Mentor as Role Model
"Our Stories Intersect"

Just as it did for me, the request for you to mentor may come as a complete surprise. I remember being astonished that someone would want my advice; after all, I'm just living on instinct, open for opportunities, looking for the chance to serve, and watching out for falling flowerpots. I said as much when asked to mentor, and he replied with passion, "But Corey, everyone who touches you comes away being more than they were before! And that's what I need!" I guess his passion convinced me, because here I am, many of these relationships later, and I'm still just being me, trying to do my best and dodging those flowerpots.

What did it take for that request to be made? Somehow, someone watched you. She watched the way you behaved with people. She watched you when you interacted with your friends and peers. She watched what happened when you were with the folks who work with and for you. And she liked what she saw. Her request came from admiration for the person she knows you to be. That admiration is the result of your way of being, and her desire to be like you. If only she could learn from you what you know, she would be as successful as you.

You created a Role Model for her – you are the person she wants to become. If she learns from you how to relate to others, she can be you. And that's what has sparked her request. Remember when you were small, and you told your dad or your mom, "When I grow up, I want to be just like you!" Well, she is grown up and she wants to be just like you – at least, she wants to resemble the person she sees in you.

The prime skill of this important role, Role Model, is the ability to look to one's own past experiences, and to apply them to the present situation. It's not so much that we repeat or recreate those experiences. It's more that whatever we learned shapes how we respond in the moment. It's not about telling your protégé "this is what worked for me" and having them replicate. Taking your experience out of context will not create an opening for success. It's more like saying, "This is what I learned, and this is what you can learn as well." It may be only that you've learned the right questions to ask. I say, "This is what I did and this is what I saw and these are the questions I've learned to ask, and I'd like to share those with you." And then I tell a story about what happened and how it worked. In fact, the best Role Models are storytellers, teaching from the stories of failure and success.

Being Role Model is being a storyteller. Storytelling is self-disclosure. Don't expect your protégé to act like you; ask him to learn from you. Human nature leads us to talk more about the "how" of situations, issues, concerns and problems rather than the "what" of them. If you get bogged down in the facts, the details, the how to's, your protégé will become dependent up on you for guidance and his growth will be very slow. Try to talk about the underlying causes and principles. A man I respected once told me, "Principles are timeless, practices are new; practices are many, principles are few." There is nothing new under the sun; there is merely a different frame around the picture.

So storytelling, or self-disclosure, takes what's happened to you and shares what you've learned from it, both the positive and the negative. I can see you smacking your forehead right now, thinking, "Why would I want to expose my failures? He doesn't respect me for what I've done wrong; he respects me for what I've done right!" Remember the humility of Jim Collins' enlightened leader. What's good about your failures is what you learned from them. Did you give it your all? When you failed, did you learn something and change your game? Did you quit?

TIP   TURN UP THE HEAT

What makes a great chef? Why can some people use the same ingredients as you and I use to create gourmet dishes we rave about for years?

Great chefs say what separates the best from the merely good is the skilful application of heat. The precise amount of heat at the appropriate moment for the right length of time releases the truly exciting flavours, the most succulent meals. Likewise, mistakes with heat, even subtle mistakes, yield results that are soggy, tough or burnt.

This is a great lesson for the mentor. Just about everything (and everyone!) needs heat to grow. You apply the heat. You have your hands on the controls. Refuse to be afraid of heat. Allow it to do its work.

Turn up the temperature when growth feels stalled. Apply the heat when you hear the same story a second time, crank it right up when you hear that story again!

Challenge your protégé. Remind her of her vision. Reiterate that growth appears when things that don't normally go together are mixed up and subjected to heat.

Turn up the temperature at the right time and sit back and take in the aroma.

These lessons are worth more than all our successes put together. And these lessons turn into stories that illustrate the message we want to imprint. If, as a Role Model, we are to help someone learn from how we have traveled down this road, we need to be able to describe it in a way that communicates the lesson learned – it is that learning that is valuable. Our job is to tell our own story in a way that brings value to someone else.

Years and years ago, I was outplaced – that's one of those great euphemisms that lives with "downsized," "made redundant," "let go," "made available to industry." The outplacement counselor taught me how to tell my own story. He told me that when you're selling yourself to a prospective employer, you have to be able to tell a story – not just say, I'm good at this, I've done that, these are my credentials. When you can tell a story about yourself in these circumstances, to say, "When I was confronted with this situation, here's what I did, and here's how the company benefited…" you'll be able to promote yourself, your activities and your results. So I built a framework for telling my own story, and had huge results. Remember "CART": Circumstances, Action, Result, Take-Away Tell your story around this formula – what were the circumstances? What did I do about it? What was the outcome? What did I learn?

C – Circumstances

- Describe the circumstances. Outline what the situation was like. Be sure to describe it with energy and interest.
- Set the stage for the story that is to come. Give the story and the lesson some context, so the content has meaning.
- Give enough detail to make the story come alive, but not so much detail that the listener gets bogged down. I have a friend who is obsessed with detail – the more the better. Sometimes when I listen to him, I want to shout, "Just cut to the chase!" Do I really need to know the exact time and date the event occurred, how he got there, what he was wearing…you get my drift? Be focused, succinct, and key in on the important points.
- Be sure to talk about how you were feeling throughout your story. The story is as much about finding a remedy for that feeling as it is about resolving the issue. The word emotion includes motion or movement. It's emotion that drives behavior, not the other way around. So when you talk about your emotions, it gives your protégé permission to feel what they are feeling, to notice it and to search for its cause. Sometimes we treat the symptom and not the cause. Identifying how you feel and the source of that feeling could put a different perspective on things. Treating the symptom guarantees

a return of the problem. Treating the cause results in a cure.

A – Action

- Describe what you actually did. Don't make it up to make it sound better – exaggeration always rings false.
- Begin, if you can, with a short description of what you considered doing, and then talk about why you chose the course of action you did. It could be a pro and con discussion, or a look at the ripple effect of each option available to you, or a discussion about what you wanted to do versus what you chose to do. This helps your protégé understand that the choice may not always be clear, and that thinking and preparing can assist not only in making the right choice but also in creating the confidence she needs to carry it through.
- Describe the specific actions you took.
- Include your emotions in your story. Were those emotions the ones you expected, or did you anticipate different feelings? Did your emotions affect your intended behavior and change it? Were your emotions a result of what you anticipated would happen, or a response to how the other person showed up?

R – Result

- Then talk about what happened. Were you able to resolve the issue? It doesn't really matter whether or not a solution was created. Your listener will draw his own conclusions about how your story applies to him, and will anticipate his own results.
- Ensure that in this part of your story, you give him sufficient information to intuit the upcoming "takeaway" without actually saying it. The story should have led him to an understanding of why you're telling it before you explain your reasons.
- Don't forget the emotional quotient. How did you feel about the resolution? Were you satisfied? Curious?

Angry? Disappointed? Encouraged? Open the door to further discussion about your satisfaction or disappointment – this helps your listener to discern what he is expecting from his action. Knowing what is expected and being prepared for something different gives him greater control over the results and his response to those results.

T – Takeaway

- Talk about what you learned. Were you pleased with the outcome? Did the action go the way you had planned? What were the barriers and the factors contributing to your success?

- What did you learn about yourself? Knowing and understanding yourself is the first step in leading others, and as human beings we are always changing, transforming. No event is the same as any other event because it's never happened in this time, with these people, under these circumstances. It's always new, and there is always something new to learn.

- What will you do differently in the future? Knowing what you know now, how could it look if you chose to go again, to make a new attempt at resolution?

- Now ask your protégé if she has any insights into her own situation now that she's heard your story. Find out her interpretation. What is she hearing from her internal voice? What story did she hear you tell – I guarantee it will be different from the one you think you told. It's essential to check in to verify that the message heard is the one you intended. If it's not, you get to go again. It's easy to think we have all the answers, and that the answers are intuitively obvious. They're only obvious to us – everyone else is oblivious until we can make ourselves clear.

So you can see the formula I've created. Now let me illustrate this with a story of my own.

I find that most leaders, just like most people, really don't like confrontation. We all shy away from it, usually to our detriment. As I sat one day with my protégé, it became apparent that he needed to confront the destructive behavior of one of his team members. As he talked, I sensed that he could only see negative consequences resulting from such a confrontation.

Having been there myself, I shared a story of a pivotal time in my leadership career when the attitude and approach of a senior member of my team was creating tremendous discord within the team. I knew I had to have a courageous conversation with the team member. I prepared for that meeting, understanding that when I gave up my desire to keep everyone happy, and focused instead on doing the right thing (including letting the team member go if that was the only solution), I felt confident and free about having that meeting.

Then I described how the meeting went; we never actually finished our conversation because the team member became very emotional. What I was saying landed for her; she was totally unaware of the impact she was having. From that day forward, she was a new person, and the team began to function again!

My purpose in the story was not to promote myself as an excellent problem solver, but to illustrate that confrontation doesn't have to produce a negative outcome. In fact, like bodybuilders tearing down muscle fiber and resting in order to rebuild and come back stronger the next time, confrontation is often necessary and it can work for good.

Let's debrief this through the CART model. The Circumstances I described were the team member's behavior and the state of the team. My Action was preparing for and having the courageous conversation. The Result was an emotional team member, a new outlook and a dramatic improvement in the harmony of the team. The Takeaway was the potential benefit of confrontation, rather than the fear of conflict. It works!

Let's recap.

Storytelling is not about you! It is about your protégé and his forward progress.

Even when the details of your story are very interesting (or flattering) tell only enough to get to the takeaway. If you so burden them with detail that they are thinking about you rather than about them, you've missed an important opportunity!

It is highly unlikely that you will know that you will be sharing a specific story at a specific mentoring encounter. That means you will often tell stories without having prepared them. So, as you get inspired with the perfect example, keep CART in mind. Remember that the reason you tell the story is to get to the T – the takeaway. Be sure to set the story up to deliver your message clearly.

When I am mentoring, I often rehearse with my protégé. I have them practice telling their stories in preparation for telling someone else, tying it up to the CART framework. That way, they don't get caught in the role of raconteur, which is a misuse of everyone's time.

And what's our takeaway from all of this? The best Role Models are the storytellers. And that storytellers don't say, "Watch what I do!" nor do they say, "Do what I say!" They say, "What can you learn from this experience I've had?" And then they slip into the other roles to reinforce and support the stories they've told.

You are the **Role Model**. Reflect on your past with a sense of thankfulness. The victories, the mistakes, the lessons you have learned make a genuine difference in your protégé's life. Someone very special looks to you; smile back and look ahead. Be worthy as the **Role Model**.

Dear Journal:

Andy and I are reaching a point in our journey where he's traveling uncharted territory - at least within his experience. How exciting to be able to guide an eager, ambitious apprentice down a path he has not yet traveled!

Andy has been telling me where he wants to go in his career. I'm glad of two things: one, he knows what he wants! And two, the places he wants to go are familiar to me! I know the route he's taking, and I can show him the shortcuts and the quicksand.

I don't want to do all his work for him. If I do, he'll get where he wants to go but he won't be able to retrace his steps, let alone guide someone else. I have to be careful not to be a caretaker - I want to direct and guide, but not to lead. And I want him to know the accomplishment is all his.

After all, mentoring is not just about helping Andy to have success. It's about leaving a legacy in terms of paying it forward - passing on to someone else the gift of guidance he has received.

Andy and I are going on safari!

Chapter Five

The Mentor as Guide
"What's My Next Step"

Have you ever read stories about the men and women who set out to conquer the highest, most challenging mountains in the world? We hear about trips to the top of Mount Everest or K2: the preparation, the physical training, and the challenges of weather and lack of oxygen. Critical decisions must be made about how much equipment to carry, about whether to take oxygen tanks and be held back by the weight, or whether to tough it out on one's own lung power in the hopes of a quicker ascent to the top.

What's amazing to me is that not one of these expeditions could survive without the help of the Sherpa guides. These are men whose life consists of guiding, coaching and supporting members of the expeditions up and down the mountain face, without benefit of the equipment, oxygen, training and financial support that the visiting climbers bring. Trekking up the mountain is another workday for the Sherpa. Born and bred in the mountains, they're accustomed to the air, the climate, and the vagaries of the weather. Having made the trip so many times, the routes are familiar, almost comfortable.

No climber wishing to reach the summit would consider taking the risk of not hiring a guide to take him or her through the dangerous process. Trophy hunters on safari in the savannah engage a guide for two reasons: to show the places most likely to harbor wild animals and to keep the expedition out of harm's way. Fishermen venturing into the Rocky Mountains hire native fishing guides to show them which island to paddle to, which rock outcropping to reach by nightfall, where the rapids are on the river and how to navigate them. And even those who are visually challenged rely on guide dogs to help them navigate the obstacles in the street that we take for granted.

The path on which the mentor takes the protégé is internal, leading him into himself, facilitating growth. Your focus as a Guide is to guide his path, not yours. Even though you may have walked this way many times, this journey is not yours; the obstacles and the rewards may not be when or where you expect. Be prepared to be flexible, and remember the protégé will learn to the degree you allow him to experience events along the way.

Most of what you see will be familiar. Dig into your experience and point out the way for your protégé. Some of what you say will be storytelling. Most of what you say will be focused on her and her current situation. You don't have to prove yourself here; trust has been established and your word is your worth.

The journey the protégé is setting out to take may seem daunting to him and to you. A wise person once said, "Mile by mile, it'll take a while; yard by yard it can be hard; inch by inch, it's a cinch." My version of that maxim is the corny old joke: How do you eat an elephant? One bite at a time!

As Guide, it's very important for you to break your instructions into bite-sized pieces (no pun intended; well, maybe). People need to know that what is in front of them can actually be accomplished, and they need to have frequent, small victories. Accomplishing an interim goal does two things. It keeps the protégé motivated through a system of effort, success and reward. It also lets the protégé see that she is on the right path – achieving what she set out to achieve, knowing that the greater goal is just a little bit closer.

Most goal-setting programs advise you to make "SMART" goals – Specific, Measurable, Achievable, Realistic, and Time Related. This applies to each goal set – not just the big dream your protégé wants to achieve, but yearly, quarterly, monthly, weekly goals too. And especially goals that can be accomplished between one mentoring meeting and the next.

When you show a novice climber a mountain and expect her to get to the summit, you've given her a task that is overwhelming. When you point out an outcropping of rock a few hundred yards away, she sees the immediate possibility of reaching that rock, and may even feel exhilarated about the prospect of getting there.

Baby Steps, Grown Up Accomplishments

Little steps lead to big objectives. It's important for your protégé to see that your directions will help him reach the destination you have agreed upon together. Like a roadmap, he needs to see that he is making progress.

It's also your task to prepare him for what might happen in the future. Together, you try to anticipate the potholes, roadblocks, detours and blind corners that might confront him. When possible, consider together what action might be taken on those occasions.

One tool I like to use in this way is a classic business model called the SWOT analysis. SWOT stands for Strengths, Weaknesses, Opportunities and Threats. Useful for any size organization, I also find it very helpful in guiding a protégé, especially if I am not familiar with the field in which she works. The strengths and weaknesses are internal – that which is significant in the individual. Your protégé must be acutely self-aware of her skills and abilities, the qualities that make her unique. She must also be aware of those areas in which she should seek outside assistance.

I've never subscribed to the philosophy that one should focus his development work on his weaknesses. I believe that each of us is created perfect, whole and complete. We live in a world of comparison, always searching for the areas of excellence and areas of deficiency that can only be measured by a standard against someone else.

Why not focus on the things we are excellent at doing? I have found that the things we do well hardly seem like work. Many people downplay their strengths. They find the tasks at which they excel so easy, they either think that everyone else is able to perform to the same level, or they think that the task must not be valuable because it so easy.

Similarly, people struggle with the things they are not excellent at doing, and look in wonder at those who find them easy. Listen to this story – maybe you'll see yourself in it. My wife tells me I am a little disorganized – okay, a lot! In fact, what she sees as a messy office, I call my efficient "piling system." Seriously, if I know the approximate date of a document, I know where to find it in the pile! And I know that it's in the pile!

My wife has the gift of organization. So every now and then she visits my office and satisfies her need to organize – and for weeks afterward I have to call her every time I'm looking for something.

Now I would NEVER want to BE like my wife. I've watched her suffer in the midst of chaos, and not be able to relax until order is restored. But I certainly value this characteristic in her, and I couldn't live without it in my life.

So what I do is do what I do best – create, write, coach, speak, train, pile! And I let my wife do what she does best – organize, file, sort, tidy, create structure and pattern, plan. Together, using our strengths, we get the job done efficiently and effectively.

That's a long-winded story to illustrate my philosophy. Develop your strengths, what you're REALLY good at, find someone who does well what you don't, and get them to do it for you!

The other two parts of the SWOT analysis, Opportunities and Threats, have to do with external influences – what's out there that shows great opportunity and potential for your protégé as she pursues her goals, and what dangers or obstacles exist that could slow her down, get in her way or possibly sabotage her progress.

If you can create this kind of map with your protégé, you'll have together created the plan for success, and you will have a sound process for anticipating the things that could derail the plan.

TIP

PAY ATTENTION

Mentoring conversations are rich. They are full of content, emotion, possibility and heart. There is so much we want to remember. The temptation is to write things down – resist it!

Mentoring is about paying attention. It's about being fully present, a live and active in the immediate conversation. Making notes can be as distracting as looking over the person's shoulder to see who else is in Starbucks with you, or repeatedly checking your watch as if something else is more important. Remember, this conversation is not about you.

I submit that you make a few notes immediately after the session if you need to remember something. Perhaps even use a digital recorder to help you remember important pieces of the conversation. If you must make a note, please write no more than four words – just enough to spark your memory without removing yourself from the dialogue for very long.

There are two exceptions to this principle. During the actual conversation, I suggest that you put pen to paper when you hear the protégé use an "emotion" word (frustrated, excited, tired, energized, bored, hurt, overwhelmed, etc.). Jot it down to remind yourself to come back to the feeling. You don't want to forget but you must remain present. Eventually you will say something like: "you used the word "energized;" what did you mean by that?"

The other acceptable time to write something down is when the protégé makes a commitment to action. I often ask: "So, can I write that down?" which gives the coming action a sense of permanence.

The bottom line is, try not to take notes. Even the paper between you can get in your way. Think about it, when someone writes something down that you have said, you replay that moment and may miss the next one.

The more fully engaged you are in the dialogue, the more you will remember what really matters.

Check In, Let Go

As you travel this path, check in with your protégé along the way. Find out what he is learning. Learn to ask him what options he is considering – you may not have to be vigorous in your direction. You may find that he is moving in the direction you want him to go, and you can confirm, rather than guide, his movements. This will happen more and more as you spend time together living in the possibilities of the future.

The mentor's temptation is to be controlling. It would be so wonderful (and so self-serving) to direct the process, like a film or theatrical director, in the wings, taking credit at the final curtain call for the work and skill of the actors on the stage. RESIST! What you are doing must be done in your protégé's best interest. This is all about him. Remember the story about standing on the shoulders of giants? No fingerprints! If you guide every step, no learning will take place, and there will be no legacy.

Your objective as Guide should be to get out of this role as quickly as you can. People grow faster when they design, choose and execute for themselves.

In fact, guiding is a place you visit when necessary, but you don't stay there long. Your task is to help him develop navigational skills, not just to help him achieve short-term objectives.

Ask the question "Why am I suggesting this?" every time you make a suggestion. Ask her to repeat the instructions in her words to imprint the forthcoming action on her psyche. Let her figure out the answer herself – the light will go on, and the connection will be made. The neural pathway will be formed, and the next trip down that path will lead to the right conclusion – because you created the experience of understanding, rather than just pointing in the right direction.

You should Guide only when your protégé truly doesn't have the wherewithal to move down this path by herself. Guard against being an easy way out; you can't become the planner for her. Ask the question, "What do you think?" so many times that she anticipates and answers it before you even ask. Your plan for her is to teach her how to plan; that's all.

Then have her 'commit' to the action herself. "You've heard my suggested plan of attack. What are you going to do? How will that generate progress?" Her answers will lead her to the commitment for action, fully understanding what she is committing to, and being ready because of the preparation you've encouraged.

What Happened?

When you de-brief a guided journey, much of the discussion should be about what your protégé is learning about charting his course. The process of mentoring is to experience only once – we learn from everything we do. So your protégé not only learns specifically about the event he just went through, he learns how to apply it to a variety of other instances, because that's where you guide him to look. Every subtlety of an event or task should be re-examined in the macro view. "If we were looking at this event through a video recording, what would we see? What didn't we see, that if we could have seen, would have prevented us from falling into the trap?"

The guide not only directs where to go to avoid obstacles, but also does an after-action review of exactly what went down – because we sure don't want to do that again! And one day, when we are mentoring someone else, we could help her avoid the same obstacle.

Most importantly, the mentor as Guide is really a signpost. The protégé has her route mapped out and she knows where she's going. She watches for the signs along the way confirming her progress, and when she gets off track, she stops to ask for directions. Maybe the 'mentor as gas station attendant' is an appropriate analogy?

You are the **Guide**. You have traveled this way many times. You hold the secrets to traversing the terrain of success. You know the path to the future and can provide safe passage to those who trust your advice. You are the **Guide**.

Dear Journal:

Andy and I had a big revelation today! We discovered that:

You don't know what you don't know!

I know that sounds corny and it somewhat smacks of common sense, but it hit home as we talked and I realized that Andy didn't have any idea what I was talking about! We discovered a hole in his experience that needs to be filled, and it will take some tutoring to fill it.

Andy thought that he had all the tools he needed to achieve his goals, but he couldn't see what was missing because he wasn't aware that it was important.

So I'll have to bone up on some skills I've taken for granted. It takes a lot more knowing when you have to teach someone else. Sometimes I do things intuitively, but I couldn't tell you how I know that they need to be done or why. I'll have to figure this out, come up with an explanation and create a list of resources.

The best way for me to serve Andy now is to point him in the direction of some credible information. I wonder what his learning style is - he doesn't do much talking and he seems to understand best when I create diagrams and flow charts, so he's probably a visual learner. I'll need to look for some videos and models and give him some homework applying what he's learning.

This is beginning to be fun!

Chapter Six

The Mentor as Tutor
"Lifelong Learners Make
the Best Teachers"

Albert Einstein once said, "The significant problems we face in life cannot be solved at the same level of thinking we were at when we created them." You'll probably need to read that one out loud a couple of times before you really get it – I know I did!

What he's really saying is that the challenges that face us arise because there is some knowledge, skill or ability lacking in what we're doing. If we possessed what we needed, the problem would not have been created. Only by learning the part that's missing can we resolve the problem.

We need a tutor to help with that. Learning and changing my game have helped me to overcome every obstacle I faced. Some of the changes I was able to effect by myself. But there were times when only the help of a mentor who taught me what I needed to know enabled me to get past the barriers.

The area that opens up the biggest possibility is the zone of things that we don't know that we don't know. Oblivious, unaware, blissfully ignorant, we drift through our days content. But when we start to examine what lurks in the zone of not knowing, or when what we don't know is drawn to our attention, how can we ignore that opportunity to grow?

When facing issues in life that stump us, that seem insurmountable, that are "outside our ken", we've got some major learning to do. And we need someone to teach us. So the mentor, as well as being a Sage, Role Model, Confidante and Guide at times becomes a Tutor.

It's incumbent upon the mentor to provide for the protégé what he needs to learn in order to move ahead on his journey.

The Tutor facilitates learning. This can mean directly teaching a concept, idea or technique. It can mean directing your protégé to a book, tape, course or other source that will deliver the needed learning. Regardless, you, as the mentor, must have a solid grasp of the information being reviewed or learned. You must know what's appropriate for your protégé in the particular circumstance. And you must be able to discuss the learning gained from the resource material after the fact.

Your first task in this role is to help him see his need for learning in a particular area. It's always best if he brings the gap or lack into the conversation by himself – then the learning becomes his idea. Of course you have seeded the idea about the missing knowledge. He has come to realize that he needs it. Resist the temptation to take credit for raising the subject. When he owns the need for learning, he's far more likely to put energy into acquiring it.

Often you have to spend time in the gap, exploring it, before she is ready to accept the fact that she is missing something and needs to learn. Then she will be ready for your advice about where to acquire the knowledge/skill/ability she needs.

Whew! "Do I have to start a whole program of learning for myself, just so I can mentor someone else?" you ask. All I can say is that you'd better darn well know what you're talking about. After all, that's why your protégé came to you – you're the source when he needs to learn. Your job is to teach, or to redirect to the right resource.

I once heard a politician say that the role of a political party office is to help its members be fifteen minutes smarter than the general public. That makes sense to me. I felt the same way when I was bringing up my teenagers. I had to stay one step ahead, be fifteen minutes smarter. I didn't need to know everything. I just needed to appear to know everything. And I needed to be ready.

So you don't have to be way down the road with your protégé. You just need to be two chapters ahead in the book you've recommended. Being a step ahead gives you confidence in your ability to lead.

Don't forget, your mentoring experience is really a journey the two of you take together. You travel with your protégé as he grows in knowledge and experience. You're able to talk with him about what's been learned, and you're learning again, this time from a different perspective.

If you're recommending books, videos or resources of which you already have knowledge, be sure to review them briefly at the same time your protégé is using them. This will not only keep you current on the information. It will also allow you to get perspective from the shoes of your protégé. You will be able to glean from the content the special flavor that belongs to your protégé.

Learning Together

Now, I don't want this to appear burdensome. It's not necessary for you to know everything about everything. It's a good idea to know something about most things, and to know where to go for the source information. Most of the knowledge gaps that need to be filled will be similar to the ones you filled on your journey. You have only to cast your mind back – where did I go for that information? What's new in the field that I can use?

If you have the skills and/or knowledge that your protégé is lacking, teach them yourself. When engaged in the teaching or tutoring mode, try to limit the didactic form of teaching – lecture, direction, pontificating (you probably don't do that, but I've caught my self holding forth as if I were an expert on several occasions). As much as possible teach by question and answer rather than just dumping what you know into the mind of your protégé. Questioning draws out what the learner already knows, and helps to build knew knowledge on top of a strong foundation of existing knowledge.

Much of the time you will direct them to another resource for learning – a book, a tape or CD, a seminar, a website, or other form of learning. Be sure to recommend the information you are familiar with and have respect for. Try not to guess at the quality or effectiveness of the media you recommend. There are as many different sources of information as there are people willing to provide it, and a web presence or a glossy brochure does not necessarily indicate quality information. Recommend what you know. Recommend what others you trust recommend. Scan things yourself if you have no first hand knowledge.

Continuous learning is essential for you if you take on a mentoring role. Even though we know "there is nothing new under the sun", there's always a new technique, a new style, a new buzzword to be aware of that will help your protégé stay up-to-date and on the cutting edge. You teach best what you are also learning. Learn along with your protégé.

Bring Learning to the Surface

Learning is only beneficial if you can make it stick. Have a mechanism for anchoring ongoing learning. This might mean that you ask your protégé to bring one great idea from the book she is reading to your next meeting for dialogue. You might ask her to maintain a learning journal, reflecting on what she has learned both from her activities, your discussions and specifically from the resources you have recommended to her. And you might ask pointed and specific questions about the material reviewed in order to tutor her through the application of that learning to her own situation. Your discussions while in the teaching mode must also be about having the protégé recognize that he is learning. Ask him. Push him. Try to link the learning back to something he is working   on right now. "How does it apply?" "How are you better equipped to deal with this situation now that you have this newfound knowledge?" "What would you have done in the past, in other   situations, if you had acquired this information earlier?"

People Learn Their Own Way

It's important to be aware of different learning styles. The golden rule tells us to treat other people the way we want to be treated. That means treating others with respect, generosity, kindness, humility…the list goes on. Unfortunately, it also often means that we think everyone else is like us. Of course we know that's not true; otherwise most of us would be redundant. So I recommend a slight revision to our golden rule: treat others the way they would like to be treated.

Many times someone has recommended that I use a particular written medium, and I've sat down to read, and read the same passage over and over again. Only when I finally read it out loud does the passage begin to make sense. You see, I am an auditory learner. I learn best by listening, and by speaking out loud.

In school, I hardly needed to study. As long as I attended class, listened to the lecture, and jotted some notes to solidify the learning, I was gold. When I did study, I read my notes out loud to myself. I learn so much from public radio and training CDs while I'm driving my car.

So the written word would not be my first choice, but what a disservice I would do to my protégé if I were to automatically recommend audio books, CDs and tapes for learning purposes without attempting to discover which learning style she preferred. If I recommend the wrong media, her learning process will be slower. That experience may lead her to become reluctant or even resistant to the recommended action. I need to assess what's needed and wanted in terms of her learning style. I then need to remind her of her goals, and give them back to her with the learning tasks attached.

Find out about the different learning styles – visual, auditory and kinesthetic, and learn to discover which style your protégé prefers. You can hear it in her language, you can see it in the way she records your conversations. She may even be self-aware and be able to advise you of her needs.

Don't Stall

Finally, watch for inertia. Some people believe they need to be experts before they attempt to apply what they've learned. I once had a client who, in spite of competently performing the tasks he was assigned in a specialized bureau, was convinced that he was unqualified and therefore unable to do the job until he received certification through training. Never mind that he was eminently skilled and capable at the task. Somehow the certification took root as proof of competence, and his confidence was never fully realized until he received the training.

If your protégé is anything like that, you'll experience resistance as you press him to move ahead. Understand that there will never be a perfect time to try out new skills and abilities. I always think of now as the 'second best time'. What I mean is that the best time to learn or know something was always a while ago – last year, last month, yesterday when I was messing up. And the second best time is now – because there will never be a better time. Opportunities pass. You may have other opportunities, but never again will you have the one that faces you. What will be the cost of missing this opportunity?

Army strategists say that 'a good plan executed now is better than the perfect plan never executed'. So having a "fairly good" grasp of things now is better than a complete grasp of things at some undefined time in the future. Think of it as "just in time" learning – we learn as we need to know.

And watch out for excuses – "I don't know how" is another way of saying "I don't want to". Legitimate lack of knowledge can be a barrier to progress and needs to be addressed. However, you may hear lack of knowledge as an excuse for inaction, a way of avoiding responsibility, or a way of escaping fear. I've heard a lot of clients rationalize about their situation. Know how I spell rationalize? "Rational lies". All those lies sound rational to me, but to whom are they lying? Get your deception detectors going and don't let your protégé get away with avoiding. She's depending on you!

You are the **Tutor**. You have unmined depths of information longing to be brought to light. Take a journey of discovery with your protégé. Your ability to nurture growth is clear; that's why you've been sought out. Your protégé respects the knowledge you have and is thirsty. Slake her thirst. You are the **Tutor**.

Dear Journal:

Andy has really taken to being mentored. He's moving faster than ever before, and he's sometimes ahead of me in figuring out the impact of the choices he's making. Right now, my role seems to be to encourage him to keep on going!

He needs a little prodding now and then to make a move - procrastinates on a decision or two, and then I have to push him to get some action.

And he's gotten a little big for his britches at times; I've had to rein him in a little. One thing I'll say for Andy: he's coachable and he's always willing to be coached. He doesn't take offense when I tell him the truth about his impact. His own intent doesn't confuse him.

It takes a humble and mature individual to recognize that people are judged by their impact, not by their intentions. That's a tough lesson to learn, but man! It's valuable. And people don't always want to hear what you have to say.

I'm being really careful about how I treat Andy - I have to be tough on him about getting things done, but I also want him to know how excited I am about what he's doing and how far he's come.

I'm really proud of the progress Andy has made!

Chapter Seven

The Mentor as Coach
"Even the Pros Have a Coach"

I love popcorn, and the best excuse for popcorn is a movie, so I watch a lot of movies. My favorites are the ones that focus on team coaches who drive their disadvantaged and challenged teams to victory in the face of daunting odds. **Hoosiers, Remember the Titans, Coach Carter** – all these teams had coaches who were committed, focused, driven and who stood in a place of solidarity for their teams.

What struck me about these films was the significant role that the coach played in the success of the players. The players set the goal – and the coach's task was to stay focused on the goal and get the players through the season while creating optimal performance.

The players had raw skill, and the coach turned that raw skill into finely tuned performance. The players had dreams of victory, and the coach turned those dreams into reality through hard work and perseverance. The players sometimes lost drive or focus through the season, and the coach pulled them back from their distractions. The players got lazy, and the coach pushed them to work harder. The players were tempted to take shortcuts, and the coach reminded them of the value of integrity, commitment and teamwork. In short, the coach held the team together.

The strength of a good coach lies in being able to see what's wanted and needed by the person he or she is coaching. Knowing when to push and when to hold back. Knowing what resources to pull out when the player is ready. Knowing when to teach and when to let the player experiment, because every player is different.

It's the same with mentoring – the mentor is often the Coach. We put our protégé through some drills, having him practice, giving him homework between sessions, asking questions, testing, watching performance, and above all, giving encouragement, support and a little bit of discipline whenever it's necessary.

What's at Stake for You?

The Coach is much more than a consultant. The Coach has a stake in the outcome for the one being coached. The Coach is serious about his time and effort spent maximizing the performance of the player.

I see it this way. As a golfer, I would love to improve my play so that my handicap was reduced, ideally from 19 to 12. So, if I call my golf pro, what does he say? "Come see me for a weekly lesson, work on your grip and your alignment and your takeaway and you should see some improvement by the end of the season. It will only cost you $75 per hour per lesson."

Do you see the picture? I would only buy his time. He won't be invested in whether or not I became a 12 handicap. As soon as our lesson ended, he'd fold up his clipboard and move on to the next client. He'd have nothing at stake.

I wonder what would happen if, when I first make my request, he asked what it would be worth for me to reach that 12 handicap? What if he said, "I'll help you become a 12, at which point you'll pay me $2000." That's a lot of money, but if I want this improvement badly enough...hmmm.

Think about it – what would it be like to take his offer? Now he's got something to prove, I think. He's not just going to give me a lesson and tell me to come back next week. Nooooo! He's going to make sure I practice. He's going to call me up when he hasn't seen me at the range for a few days. He's going to play a number of rounds with me to help me with my course management. He's going to cheer me on when I do well, and point out ways to improve along the way. He's now invested in what I'm becoming. He has something real at stake. His reward is based on the outcome, not on the time spent. He's going to want to get the job done well, and in a timely fashion, and he's going to make sure I perform or he won't get paid.

The football and basketball coaches in those movies I watch are in the same boat – if their teams don't perform, who gets fired? You guessed it, the Coach! So they have a stake in what goes on both on and off the field, and they're totally committed. It's like looking at your bacon and eggs – the chicken was involved, but the pig was committed!

Hold that thought – this is the mentor as Coach. You and your protégé are involved with each other – you're not just getting together for a coffee. You are both focused on improving the effectiveness of one.

Coaching Essentials

The Coach brings accountability, discipline and motivation to the relationship. It's up to the Coach to design the drills and ensure that they are completed properly. It's the Coach who pats the player on the back when things are going well, and it's the Coach who pokes the player with a stick when things are lagging. It's the Coach who creates motivation; it's the Coach who challenges excuses. It's the player who gets the glory; it's the Coach who gets the satisfaction.

So here is some advice on what's essential in coaching:

1. Coach only into a request for coaching. Yes, you have been asked to mentor, and yes, you have the right to be frank and "in your face" about what's going on for your protégé, but you still need permission to enter into these discussions. Many a relationship between mentor and protégé has been fatally injured when one or the other takes offence to what has been said, and it's usually because what's been said has been said without invitation. So it goes. "May I ask you a question about that?" "Are you willing to look at that?" "Would you like

to walk this through to its natural conclusion?" Your protégé will know what's coming, and that's perfect!

2. Stay neutral. Remember – this is not about you! I have to remind myself over and over again. It's easy to get hooked into a conversation about being right. That conversation has never served anyone well. You have a stake in the outcome, but only if the protégé finishes the course. It may be your opinion, but it's her choice. Years ago I heard a profound statement – "Good decisions come from experience; experience comes from bad decisions." She'll make some bad choices and you'll get some coaching experience because of those choices. Stay with her and walk it out.

3. Listen for commitment. Once the request has been made, the protégé may have second thoughts about his commitment to the journey. Where there is no commitment, challenge. Provoke. Get clear on what it is he wants to have happen, and how he's going to get there. And keep him accountable to that commitment – short term and long term.

4. Straight talk. A lot of mentoring relationships are damaged by what we call 'cordial hypocrisy' – the art of withholding what we really think in favor of being nice, or getting along. Your protégé will not benefit from you wanting to spare her feelings or sugarcoat your observations. As a Coach, you get to be relentless. Be honest and frank, and then listen.

5. Listen for underlying conversations. What is it that he is avoiding? What's he holding back? Is there sarcasm, apathy, discouragement in his voice? Is he saying what he really thinks? These are some of my favorite questions: "What's the conversation you don't want to have?" "What is it that you don't want me to know?" "You say you don't know – if you *did* know, what would it be?"

6. Stand 100% responsible for producing the result. You have to take a stand. Not a position – that's something you could get trapped in. A stand is for results, whatever that looks like, and however the two of you decide to get there. Have you ever heard the expression "putting a stake in the ground"? In the olden days (yes, even before I was born!) the Native Americans would go to war, tribe against tribe. And the bravest warrior would approach the enemy camp, and would tie a rope to his ankle, the other end tied to a stake. He would drive the stake into the ground, and he would not then be able to escape. Even if he wanted to run, he was bound by the stake to fight to the death. That's what it means to put a stake in the ground – to stand for producing the result you have said you will create.

7. Authentically care about the person you are mentoring. You must be able to see his potential and truly desire to see him succeed. You can coach past many stumbles when you have a genuine liking and respect for the one who is stumbling.

8. Put the coaching in their lap. "You asked me to help, and we made an agreement." The definition of promise, according to **Noah Webster's 1828 Dictionary** is "*a declaration written or verbal made by one person to another, which binds the person who makes it either in honor, conscience, or law to do or forbear a certain act. A declaration that gives the person to whom it was made a right to expect or claim the performance or forbearance of the act.*" You, as the mentor, have the right to claim performance of your protégé. "I'm responsible, and you're going to do it!"

> ### TIP PUT YOUR MONEY WHERE YOUR MOUTH IS
>
> *One of the biggest traps mentors fall into is having a great discussion about the current reality, even a solid conversation about options open to the protégé and then nothing happens!*
>
> *A mentor must ask them what they intend to do. Specifically. An effective mentor will never leave a meeting without a commitment to some specific action that will take their protégé a little way further down the road.*
>
> *Watch out here! The temptation may for the protégé to commit to an outcome that is beyond their current reach in the time they are considering. Break it down into bite-sized pieces. Committing to something doesn't have to mean finishing the whole initiative - it just means identifying a specific action that can be completed and reported the next time you meet.*

Agree on Something Important

Like playing a musical instrument or becoming proficient in a sport, practice is the key to getting better at what you do. The Coach sparks the desire to practice. He may design the drills, he may set certain targets, he may prescribe a time period for practice, etc. What is important is for the Coach to ensure that this part of the growth plan is worked.

The behavioral contract really answers the question, "Who will do what by when?" It is a specific declaration about what is going to happen, and accountability through an enforceable consequence. So when your protégé says she will complete a task before your next meeting – is there an enforceable consequence? Is she at stake for her progress, just as you are?

So the Coach sets up the drills, the practices – the behaviors. The protégé agrees and commits, making a specific declaration about what she will do. And together, you decide what will happen if it doesn't get done. Maybe she buys the coffee the next time, or visits her mother-in-law – you know, something really painful that she'll want to avoid. It's not about the consequence, really. It's about the fact that there is one and she'll have to accept it if she fails to complete the task.

It takes work to become stronger and more proficient. There will be times when the work doesn't get done. Then listen for the justification, the rationalization. The Coach needs to know the difference between an excuse and a reason. And the truth is, even the reasons lack strength when compared to the commitment that was made.

I have a friend whose voice I hear repeatedly. He only made the comment once, but I hear it over and over, every time I'm about to wimp out – to make an excuse for not doing something, mostly because I don't want to. I create a justification – I'm too busy, I'm running out of time, something important came up, I was given a new assignment... the list is endless. And what do I hear just as I'm about to say it? I hear my friend, sitting on my shoulder, saying, "Yeah, but how committed are you to building the life you want, Corey?" Rats! Foiled again! And then I honor my commitment.

You need the behavioral contracts to cover small steps – weekly, bi-weekly or monthly progress. These measure the doing in small steps, seeking small victories and measuring progress.

You also need a larger, longer-term accountability agreement that declares for the protégé:

This is what I want.

This is what I will be accountable for.

This is the support I need.

This is how we'll know we're making progress.

And you need to keep the game plan front and center so the protégé understands how everything fits together.

The role of the Coach can be an irritant (really just the little conscience troll sitting on the protégé's shoulder), but it is necessary. Don't be afraid of this. Keep at it!

And at the same time, don't fall in love with doing this, no matter how much fun you get out of being the taskmaster. It's easy to forget the goal in the process of doing.

TIP   HAVE FUN WITH THE LANGUAGE

Words are your tools; use the sharpest ones you can find.

Often a memorable conversation occurs when I substitute a dramatically different word to illustrate the action we are discussing. For instance: I've said "obsessive" when the protégé said "passionate."

Use colourful language, aggressive language, powerful language, sappy language. Use unexpected words. Use unrelated words and phrases.

Occasionally I suggest you may even use dramatically opposite words just to open up a point. "You must feel guilty for that" when I really want them to acknowledge they can be proud.

The Real Scoreboard

Finally, don't forget the feedback loop. It's important to track and measure progress; in a mentoring relationship that's not always an easy task. We can measure increased income, or performance bonuses, or promotions. But how do you measure a change in your protégé's way of being that causes a shift in the quality of the relationships he has, both at work and in his life?

The only way is to request feedback from the people who are significant in his life. And that feedback needs to come from all angles. Asking the people for whom he works will give him good information about his performance. Asking the people who work along side him, or on projects with him, will give good information about the relationships he has with people who are helpful but may not have power or influence. And asking the people who work for him will give a clear picture of what he is committed to creating on his work teams.

The feedback question can be a loaded gun. We want to know, but when it's not what we want or expect to hear, it can send us into the death spiral. "I knew I couldn't do it! I can't believe they think that about me! That's not what I meant!" You know the story.

I see feedback as a gift. I once heard someone say that we

judge ourselves by our intent, yet we judge others by their impact. Receiving feedback tells us the impact we're having on the people within our sphere of influence. Imagine that I am interacting in what I see as a direct, frank, forthright and confident manner. Yet as I walk away, I hear the comment, "What a …!" (You can fill in the blank!) If I am never made aware that this is how they are experiencing me, how will I ever be able to change? You can't "be"ware of something you're not "a"ware of.

Once I was watching a guest speaker spend about 90 minutes discussing leadership in action. The first 45 minutes were spent espousing his own virtues – his career path, what he did to get promoted, what was significant in his life. That was just about long enough to alienate the majority of the audience. I remember thinking, "This man is a legend…in his own mind!"

Only then did he start to promote the characteristics and actions of strong leaders that make them successful – and this portion of his speech was extremely well done. He closed off by announcing that he had three years left on his contract, at which time he expected to be head of his organization! Now what do you think the audience remembered about his talk? That's right – his arrogance not his skill.

There's a delicate balance between patting someone on the back and then asking for more without creating a feeling of "nothing is ever good enough". Your child comes home with his report card showing 6 A's and 1 B. Where's your focus: on the A's or the B? Sometimes you need to praise and leave it at that. Sometimes you will want to point out how this success is a stepping-stone to something even greater.

The Coach needs to tell the protégé when her efforts are not meeting the grade. "You have to try harder." "You have to pay more attention to this area." "Stay focused." "You have to put in your time and energy if you are going to meet your expectations." It's not about the activity. The two of you can be doing a whole lot of doing. In the end it's about outcomes, results.

And a focus on results is what you have when you're in the role of the mentor as a coach. Even Tiger Woods has a Coach to help him transform from good to great. When the awards are given out, everyone has someone to thank!

You are the **Coach**. You are a winner and you've been on winning teams. You have that magical mix of advice and encouragement, and the wisdom to know when to use each. You share joy in their victories and agony in their defeats. You take pride in your players, and they honor you. You have a winning record. You are the **Coach**.

Dear Journal:

Andy told me today that as we continue our relationship, he sees in me more and more the success that he admired from day one. He said that as he experiences the lessons I'm teaching him and the guidance I give, he recognizes just how much I have learned on my own personal journey. And he recognizes and appreciates the investment I'm making in him.

I'm just humbled by the opportunity he's given me to join him in his journey.

Andy gets a little frustrated with his progress - because he's in the process he doesn't always see that he's moving forward. So I'm the cheerleader, showing him the yard lines and encouraging him, as he gets closer to the goal.

When you're in the thick of things, fighting fires, pushing doors open, climbing over obstacles and coasting down the slopes, it's often difficult to see the end. My job is to keep Andy's ultimate goal firmly fixed in my mind. One of us has to keep our eyes on the prize!

I think the transformation is finally happening. Andy is flourishing and becoming the leader he aspired to be when he first came to see me. I just need to continue to praise and promote; to help Andy to receive my positive reinforcement for what it is - acknowledgement of a job well done. Soon, Andy won't need me to tell him - he'll recognize his own accomplishments.

When that day comes I'll be thrilled, and a little bit sad.

Chapter Eight

The Mentor as Sage (Part Two) "Keep Your Eye on the Finished Picture"

My mother tells me that one way to keep one's mind active, sharp and alert is to do jigsaw puzzles. It seems that we've taken that seriously in our household. Sometimes I'll stop and put in a single piece; sometimes I'll succumb to my puzzle addiction and not be able to quit. Over the holiday seasons we always have one on the go. I'm struck by the connection between the jigsaw puzzle and the mentoring relationship.

When I do a jigsaw, I find all the edge pieces first, then put together specific identifiable parts and place them approximately where they should go within the frame of the edges. Then I add in the background – you know, the sky where every blue piece looks the same and you're sure you must have dropped a piece somewhere because it's simply not there! (of course you find it later). When I'm in the puzzle, the one thing I do to keep my perspective is to keep referring at the front of the box – the big picture, the vision, what the puzzle will look like when I'm finished. So as the mentor, I'm the box!

Building Something

After establish your relationship as Confidante, the alpha and omega of mentoring is the role of the Sage. One of you needs to keep an eye on the goal, the end result, the vision. One of you needs to anchor the protégé's development in light of the overall objective. Often the protégé cannot see the movement he has made – he's too close to the action.

Your key to success in this role is your ability to remind your protégé of her goals, to animate her vision, to make it real and show her how far she's come in realizing that vision. You help her to reflect on her path and gain insight into her future. You link the present to the future in a way that shows movement toward the goal. She has been in the thick of work, head down, fighting, pushing, moving around obstacles, redefining her path. Your guiding and mentoring keeps the picture of the clearing in her mind; you remind her of what it will look like when she reaches the peak – the vistas she will see from the summit of the mountain she has set out to conquer.

When I first meet with someone starting out on this journey, I like to ask them a question: "If we are sitting together having this conversation two years from now, what will be talking about? Two years from today, what will you have done today?" I want to get a feel for their vision, where they see themselves, what success looks like to them. And if this vision is compelling enough, many of the things that need to happen between now and then will be obvious.

Sometimes it's the magnitude of what needs to be done that is overwhelming. And we've said before, one of your tasks is to help break down those tasks into bite-sized pieces to make them less overwhelming and more manageable.

In your role as Sage there are two big things. First, you keep your protégé's vision visible, constantly in front of him. You keep showing him what he's trying to become. You use new language that is vibrant, compelling, magnetic and clear, and as he progresses, the vision gets sharper, closer, touchable. You may even hold out for him a vision that's bigger than the one he has for himself.

Second, you affirm where progress is being made and how that progress relates to the goal, the vision, the end result. If life is like a motion picture, we don't see it frame by frame when we watch it; we see the story as it unfolds. As the mentor, you drop down into your protégé's life every two to three weeks and take a snapshot, and show her where she is, help her to see her progress.

Have you ever experienced being lost in the forest, or in a

> ### TIP
>
> **WHAT'S IN A NAME?**
>
> *A logjam happens when one specific log gets stuck across the path of the river's flow. Other logs pile up behind it and create havoc immediately stopping forward motion. Skilled lumberjacks isolate the offending log and then release it to restart the flow.*
>
> *Many years ago I was taught that a problem named is a problem solved. Mentors are in a unique position to identify the specific log that halts motion for the protégé. What comes next is vital: name it. Give the problem a name. Shine a spotlight directly on it.*
>
> *This is one of the most cathartic things a mentor does. It is also one of the most rewarding because it is at these moments that you may see the lights go on in the protégé.*
>
> *The dark side is: a problem mis-named or un-named is a problem jammed. If the lights don't go on, an effective mentor will ask the protégé for a more appropriate name for the problem. Together, find a name that connects for the protégé.*
>
> *Then, watch it disappear.*

wood, or somewhere where there's no landmark for which to aim? Our tendency in this situation is to circle around until we eventually find ourselves back at the place from which we started. With no landmarks, no map, we have nothing with which to mark our progress, and nothing to aim toward.

Being Sage is like watching your protégé from the highest vantage point and giving directions – you have a different perspective, the big picture, and you can encourage them to continue on, take risks, stretch, and rest.

Have you ever been orienteering? Orienteering is an adventurous activity – some risk, lots of unknown experiences. You follow compass coordinates step by step, looking for landmarks along the way. And if you are accurate in using your compass, you come out of the wilderness to a hot meal and a warm shower.

I have a friend who takes a trip every year. She goes to Northern Ontario, gets dropped off on one side of an island, and three days later a boat arrives at the other side of the island to pick her up. The risky part is that if she's not at the rendezvous point, the boat leaves. There's no room for error. She can't get lost, can't slip and get injured – no one will come to get her. All she takes with her   is a compass, a sleeping bag and some bare essentials – matches, a knife, no food or water. And that, for her, is part of the excitement, the adventure of matching wits and skills with Mother Nature. She tells me that the risk is what's exhilarating. It's how she knows she's alive. I admire her courage. For me it's an adventure just navigating the local shopping mall parking lot.

Your role is to be a compass for your protégé, not a map. A map is created by someone who has already been where you want to go. The paths have been walked, charted, every landmark seen and recorded. You use a map when you want to go where someone else has been. But you've never been to the place your protégé wants to go. You have a sense of where it is, and you have some experience in traversing the landscape. But you cannot lead him step by step, because your context is not his context. He has different work, different players in his game, different goals he's aiming towards. A compass points him in the right direction.

The Spark

As Sage, I'm the catalyst to transformation, and sometimes this role surprises me. There's always a point in the relationship where I realize that I can't let go. It's like the point of no return. I'm the anchor – if I let go, all will be lost. I'm tempted to be fearful, to quake at the awesome responsibility I feel in this role, at this time. But I can't afford to be afraid at this point. I must keep on keeping on, regardless of resistance from my protégé, regardless of the obstacles that seem to keep on coming, regardless of the temptation to relax and let down my guard.

It's at this point I know I need to keep building the grander vision. It's when my protégé begins to get weary in well doing. I keep her eye on the prize, on her grander vision. I help her to look back to see from whence she came when the goal seems just as far away as when she started.

I learn to talk in snapshots, and in motion pictures. I find metaphors that work. I create images in her mind of what it will be like when she's reached her goal. I remind her of what she was committed to when we started out.

I review what we talked about as we worked through the *C2 Matrix: Confidence/Competence* and get a feel for the growth I have seen in my protégé both internally and externally, and remind her of these things.

TIP   BACK TO THE FUTURE

People are often so locked in the past or burdened by the present that their situation feels hopeless. The mentor is not doing a service to his/her protégé to wallow in what's already done.

Every mentoring pair must understand what the ideal future looks like. They should spend quality time at every meeting reminding themselves that the long-term objective of their relationship is tied directly to those future goals.

Do this with questions. The more the protégé verbalizes her ideal state, the more detail that it contains, the more vivid the descriptions and the conversation around it, the more compelling it becomes.

I like to take the protégé to a place a few years out. I'll ask: "Four years from today what will be different in your life? What will it feel like? Detail for me what you will be doing today."

That's the mentor's job. Keep the end in sight. All the time. Again, keep the end in sight.

The Spotlight

The Sage turns a spotlight on his actions and his growth:

- *In terms of living out his personal values.* Specific values begin to become clear in the actions he chooses. Many times people have not become clear about the core values for which they stand. And those who have indeed set values have often identified values for which they would like to stand, or which appear to be noble and honorable. But when you look at the physical universe, which doesn't lie, another set of values shows up in how they choose to behave. You can illuminate this incongruity; show your protégé the reality of what he's doing and offer him the opportunity to either shift to behavior that reflects to the values he would like to live out, or to clarify the values he chooses to demonstrate in his daily life.

- *In terms of achieving her mission.* I show her how the pieces of her puzzle fit together to show progress. Often she is so caught up in the doing that she can't see the bigger picture she's creating.

- *In terms of skills and capabilities becoming second nature.* I show him what he's doing today that he was incapable of doing when we started. I show him how the gap between goal and skill set has shrunk. I show him a vision of an unprecedented future – limitless, bounded only by his ability to identify the impossible future and then to find a way to make it happen.

- *In terms of style.* Her style is becoming more and more defined as she moves through the mentoring process. It reveals who she is. This is where I help her get to know herself, and more importantly, to get to like herself. I show her how her individual style helps her get things accomplished. I show her how important it is to own her own style; someone else's style would be taken out of context, and would show up like an ill-fitting costume. And I show her where her style can get in the way of her progress, and work with her to discover options for shifting to improve her effectiveness.

- *In terms of his goals.* I check in regularly as to how he feels he is doing with respect to his goals. Does he still know what those goals are? Are they goals still relevant? Is he making progress? I keep checking in that the goals for which he is striving are the ones that will propel him to his vision. And I emphasize the progress he is making – even if it is small, progress will keep him going. And if he has started to veer off target, I identify that as well. I'm really like a curb on the roadway – as he starts to drift, he bumps into me and corrects his course.

- *In terms of her strategies.* Are they working? What's not working? What should she stop doing? Start doing? Keep doing? I reaffirm her strategies in light of the higher objectives she has set. I check for congruency.

- *In terms of his vision* – by reminding him of what he wanted when we first started, we can begin to refine and define that vision. We find language that is more compelling – the more work we have done, the stronger his sense of direction and destination. The vision is magnetic north for him...something that he recalibrates his life, his actions and his leadership to. And I show him how what he is doing is leading him to that vision.

The spotlight I shine highlights the fact that what he is actually doing day to day, today and tomorrow, his tactics, his daily to-do lists, are the things that are moving him ahead, more than just survival, more than just the daily grind.

I am the keeper of his resolve. I listen to his frustrations about his perceived lack of progress and reassure him that there is movement.

I see what is possible.

I don't let up.

I love my protégé, and to an even greater extent, I love what she is becoming. Why? Because success is not about the doing, but about the becoming.

You are the **Sage**. You are the alpha and omega. You soar above and have the eagle's eye on your protégé's path. You have the wisdom of knowing the destination and the journey, and you are confident. Share your confidence. Feed your protégé. Strengthen and encourage. Beckon from the finish. You are the **Sage**.

Dear Journal

Hey! I just thought of something! What if, when I'm finished with Andy, someone else asks me to mentor him or her? Could I do this all over again?

Well, probably, if only I'd made some notes about what I did and how I did it. There's no point in being an unconscious competent - someone who knows what to do but not how or why. That's not marketable, or even duplicable.

So what have I done? Note to self - create an outline of the mentoring process. Start by reading your own journal, self!!!!

And don't forget to do the 360° check-up - look ahead, look back, inside, outside, look up and look around. I've discovered that being in the moment is essential to successful mentoring. You can miss an awful lot of opportunities for impact when you're not focused. I lost some valuable time with Andy in the beginning by not being focused on the purpose of our getting together.

I think I'll put together a meeting map - a guideline for mentoring sessions that I can follow consistently so that I get the most out of every session.

It's the least I can do to honor the person who has honored me with the request for mentorship.

Chapter Nine

The Conversation
"Doing the Being"

In the previous chapter, I said that the mentor's task as Sage was to be a compass for the protégé, to point him in the right direction. In this chapter, I want to give you a North Star from which to point the compass. I've created a framework for mentoring you can use as your guide, keeping you on course as you guide and direct your protégé.

The critical challenge you face each time the two of you meet is to conduct a mentoring session that is meaningful and creates impact. A framework can help you stay focused on what you want to accomplish during your time together. The framework I have built here will allow you both the freedom to operate according to your style and the confidence to know that all bases are covered.

A word of caution: This framework should not become a checklist. Rather, it should become natural, second nature, intuitive. A perception by the protégé that you're mechanically going through a series of hoops will take away the flow of the session and make it feel mechanical and disconnected.

Imagine a choir standing with their choir books, eyes on the pages and the words, singing the content. Now imagine the same choir, sans choir books, singing and swaying and dancing and pouring emotion all over the stage. Which one comes from the heart? Somehow the engagement is completely different when you're not reading from the book.

| TIP | COLOUR INSIDE THE LINES |

As you continue to meet, as you grow to know and like each other, you will discover more things that interest you and more things you want to follow up with each other. Logically, small talk may begin to overwhelm your dialogue. Small talk has its place as a warm up for a mentoring conversation just like stretches prepare athletes for the game. But on every playing field I know, no one wins anything in the warm-up.

Take the lead in making check-ins brief. Cycle back to the focus of your relationship as quickly as you can. Often a question that links the story just told with the person's stated long-term objective will snap the conversation back to productivity. Please master the temptation to dig too deeply into things that don't really matter. Showing interest in the superficial detracts from the important conversation that must follow.

This is not to counsel that a mentor be disinterested in the day-to-day life of the protégé - quite the contrary. Just practice bridging it back to the real reason you are together.

Early in your relationship, you identified how the protégé sees success for herself. Keep this the north star of your interaction.

Your connection with your protégé is your priority. Covering the content is secondary. Your relationship is created one conversation at a time. Here is what your conversation should look like.

1. Look Around
   Purpose: To check in with each other.
   > You must listen to and sense the true state of the person you are with. Listen generously. Listen to the conversation behind the conversation. Listen to the question behind the answer and the answer behind the question.

   Questions you might ask:
   - What do you want to accomplish today?
   - What is up for you today?
   - Is there anything you feel we must talk about today?

2. Look Back

Purpose: To debrief the interval since the last meeting.
You must acknowledge progress made since your last meeting. And you must hold your protégé accountable for his commitments and his performance goals. Listen for justification and rationalization in the reasons for any missed commitments or goals.

Questions you might ask:

- What actions have you taken since our last conversation?
- What did you accomplish?
- What challenges did you face?
- How did you handle those challenges?
- Have you stayed true to your commitments?
- What have you discovered through the process of honoring your commitments?

3. Look Inside

Purpose: To focus on the protégé's heart and growth.
You must ensure that growth is meaningful and lasting, not superficial. Growth that is anchored within, linked to emotion, is likely to stick. Growth that is related to task and performance doesn't always stay connected and grounded. Emotions drive behavior. If you can remain committed to a particular way of being, your behavior will consistently support that and you will experience consistent and dramatic personal and professional development.

Questions you might ask:

- Where do you need help to deepen/open?
- What challenges, concerns, achievements, or areas of learning need to be addressed?
- What gaps have you noticed in your relationships?
- What is it that you don't want to talk about?
- What's holding you back?
- What is it that you're pretending not to see?

TIP   **BOLD QUESTIONS**

Your protégé wants you to help her play a bigger game. That means trying new things, looking in new places for answers and possibilities. It means bolding going where she may not have gone before.

How?

Ask a bold question. Ask it pointedly. Ask it in as few words as you can. And wait. Wait for a response. Don't move on without one.

In my experience these questions often elicit the opening response: "That's a very good question." Or, "I've never really thought about that before." And likely they haven't. That's what gives them the power.

Some of my favorites include:
- ✓ *What are you avoiding?*
- ✓ *What's holding you back?*
- ✓ *What are you afraid of?*
- ✓ *What excuses are you making to yourself?*
- ✓ *What are you pretending not to know?*
- ✓ *What's your inner voice telling you?*

This type of question adds salt and pepper to the conversation intensifying the flavor dramatically. You'll both remember the meal.

---

4. Look Outward
    Purpose: To examine options for the immediate and long term future.

    In looking around, the protégé may have a restricted view. You must open up the possibilities available to him that are linked to his desired future. We all see the world through our own filters – your protégé may not always see what you see. Give him the opportunity to see as many options as possible so that he can truly make the best choices.

    Questions you might ask:
    - What might you do in the next (specific number of) days to move forward?

- What might you hope to accomplish?
- If you did know what to do, what would it be? (some times the "I don't know" response comes up – this question would be your response)
- Other than that, is there anything else?
- What's the second best option?
- How will this option impact your plan for your life?

5. Look Ahead
   Purpose: To establish commitments as to specific tasks.
      Specific action steps are essential to ensure this meeting has been meaningful. A mentoring session without action steps is just a cup of coffee. Get commitment from your protégé, and be clear about what is expected. Make sure you get a commitment to a task and the date by when the commitment will be met. Commitments that are clear, even written, are the ones that are met consistently. Build as much success as possible into your process.
   Questions you might ask:
   - What will be different about you in 30 days?
   - What are you going to report?
   - What will you have done that we can celebrate?
   - How will you know when you've met your commitment?
   - What are you prepared to be at stake for? What will the consequence be should you miss your target?

6. Look Upward
   Purpose: To ground the meeting and its content the protégé's own values and purpose.
      You must ensure that your protégé is on track and anticipating coming growth. The most significant content of your conversation is the last thing you talk about. That's the part that sticks, the part your protégé will remember. So as you wrap up this portion, be sure to recap what you've talked about, recap the

commitments, and close with a conversation reminding your protégé of what she committed to when you first got together. Remind her of what she said when you asked her what her dreams were. Have her write them down, the commit to them verbally with you. Hold out her purpose and commitment in front of her. Make these commitments a "get to" rather than a "have to".

Questions you might ask:

- What impact will your planned actions have on your immediate situation?
- What implications will your planned action have a year from now?
- What impact will your planned actions have on the people around you? Will there be a ripple effect? Positive or negative?
- How can I assist you?

The last question really sums up your attitude as a mentor. Imagine that your sole reason for existing is to help this person get to their unprecedented future.

Do that.

Dear Journal:

Man! I sure didn't expect that writing down my process would be so difficult, or get me so bogged down. I'm so busy "doing" that I forgot about the importance of "being"!

I guess my best thoughts are to forget about process, and to focus on way of being. After all, it's the law of sowing and reaping. My way of "being" will cause me to "do" things in a consistent way that will allow me to "have" what I want.

Therefore, if I want to "be" a mentor, I will guide, teach, coach, learn and be a role model for my protégé. In "doing" these things, I will "have" a relationship with someone who is willing to take my advice and use it. And how cool will that be!!!

The other thing I've discovered through this process is that I need to have many hats, and I have to be prepared to change my accessory at the drop of ... you guessed it...a hat!!

I need to know when to teach and when to guide, when to lead by example, when to ask questions and when to keep confidences, and I need to be able to move from one to another as needed and at a moment's notice.

That's why a model is tough to create - because the mentoring relationship is so ethereal, so dynamic, so unpredictable in its motion.

And that's why I'll definitely do this again - if I'm fortunate enough to be asked!

Chapter Ten

Being In The Moment
"Today's Conversation Could Make a Lasting Difference"

Sometimes we get so caught up in the day to day doing that we forget to step back and look at the whole picture –at the end result, where we're going, what we want to achieve. We forget to be 'in the moment', conscious of what's actually taking place right here, right now. We forget to be present in our conversation, to really hear what's being said. Instead we look to what we want to see, what we expect to hear, what we think things should look like.

Mentoring comes from within. The mentor's passion is for the growth of the protégé; he gets to share in the celebration of success, he feels the pain of setback and failure. He must be fully engaged with the protégé, all the while remaining strongly aware that now is merely a moment in time.

Mentors need to train their instinct to know when to play each of the six roles, how to shift from one role to another, and what to expect during the transition between roles.

Each role is as important as the other, and the role you choose to play at any given time is totally dependent upon what is wanted and needed right now. So, as a mentor, I check in on the role I'm playing to see if that role is serving them well. Is an example, being a Role Model, enough to mentor my protégé, or does she need more than what I'm doing right now? Is she capable of doing more, of receiving more than I'm giving?

If I'm in the role of Guide – does she need more than just direction?

If I'm in the role of Tutor – does she need more than knowledge?

As Coach – does she need more than encouragement, motivation, accountability?

And the only way to know that is to check in with my protégé – to ask. I can't just assume that I know what she needs – how arrogant would that be? In my commitment to being humble, I will assume that my protégé has an instinct for what she needs, so I'll ask. I am always looking for what's needed to come from inside my protégé.

And I always err on the side of being too tough, rather than too easy – if I'm doing all the work, she could become dependent on me – and I know she's strong enough, resilient enough and has sufficient ability to get the job done – if she didn't, she wouldn't have recognized that having a mentor would serve her. So I can push her harder and pull her harder than she thinks she can handle. It's easier to back off than to toughen up, and you'll be surprised at the level of performance that comes with stretching.

I'm Stuck

Listen for "stuckness" – I really don't know what else to call it. It happens when there's no progress, no movement. It happens when homework doesn't get done, when your protégé can't see the next step, or the vision, or the progress that's happening. People get stuck on things like focus, or direction, knowledge, motivation. Sometimes being stuck shows up as an excuse for why something wasn't or can't be done.

When you sense this "stuckness", don't dive right in to resolve it. Process it with your protégé. Say, "I sense that you're stuck on (name it). What's holding you in place? What might I say that would release the logjam?"

- If he needs to hear how you dealt with something similar, shift to Role Model
- If he doesn't know what to do, shift to Guide
- If he lacks understanding, knowledge or skill, shift to

Tutor
- If he lacks confidence, focus, discipline, shift to Coach

TIP   **A GAME TO PLAY**

Occasionally you will find that the conversation with your protégé has stalled. I use a number of approaches to restart the dialogue. One of the most effective I call "Ascribe A Feeling".

It's simple. At whatever point you are in the conversation, ascribe a specific feeling to the protégé. Say something like: "you sound angry," "you appear hurt," or "I sense that you are excited." It almost doesn't matter what you say; just be clear about the emotion you are attaching to what you've heard.

Universally, people want their feelings interpreted correctly. If you have ascribed the wrong emotion, I guarantee that your protégé will correct you. "I'm not angry, I'm frustrated." Similarly, when you have chosen the right emotion, they will validate it. "You bet your life I'm disappointed; I've wanted that for years."

Either way, the conversation has begun again. And, feelings take you to a place where growth is more likely to happen. Congratulations.

Make him ask for what he needs, but don't allow him to cop out. There's a big difference between an excuse and a reason. Sometimes, the "stuckness" is the result of a "racket" – a strategy the protégé uses to get out of something – responsibility, work, something uncomfortable or distasteful – a racket deflects the need to own up to the blockage. If it sounds like your protégé is rationalizing, call it what it is. He's just fooling himself. So discernment on the part of the mentor is important. If your protégé is using excuses, face it, deal with it and get over it.

If she is truly stuck, take the conversation away from what's not getting done and point to towards the current state of being – process that. Look for the pin that might pop the balloon. Look for the one log that's creating the log jam – find it, reposition it, or blow it up so that the river can start to move the logs again.

A big jam can happen around the whole area of confidence. Lack of confidence gets him stuck and prevents him from moving forward. Remember my friend who is extremely competent, and a quick study? He picks up knowledge and skill very easily, and is committed to excellence in everything he does. His Achilles' heel is that he is convinced that only formal training qualifies him to perform the task. So until he's taken a course, and has the certificate in hand, he's not competent. Now that's a log that can jam progress!

Lack of confidence keeps you in the present and doesn't allow you into the future. It takes confidence to go into the future – confidence and faith are very close together. I try to teach my protégé that confidence doesn't necessarily mean that he knows what or how to do something. Confidence means having faith in his experience and his instinct, and if he doesn't have the experience, I urge him to trust his own instincts.

Sometimes your protégé can get stuck when he encounters something he hasn't experienced before – that's when you put on your Tutor hat.

Occasionally the "stuckness" arises from the filters or paradigms that your protégé listens through. The universal human paradigm is that we see the world the way we think it "should" look based on our belief systems and our experiences. Each "should" is a paradigm. And those paradigms can be pretty strong – if a paradigm has hold on you (rather than you holding on to it), it may be difficult to recognize that hold – after all, that fish doesn't know it's swimming in water! So helping your protégé to recognize the paradigm for what it is, and then to determine whether or not that paradigm serves him well could be a way to reposition the log in the jam and get the logs flowing again.

Question Yourself

Remembering that the role of Confidante is part of every conversation, if you need a default role – let it be that of Coach. Try not to resort to Guide or Tutor unless that role is specifically called for in the conversation. Even then, don't make it easy for your protégé to rely on you to guide or teach if she should be doing that herself.

Remember, she does the heavy lifting, not you. You are with her on her journey; don't allow yourself to own the journey. She owns her future, not you. Listen to your inner voice. Your instincts are good when you listen with integrity as your protégé talks.

And ask questions. You may leave a conversation with a question unanswered; please don't leave a meeting with a question unasked.

TIP   I'M HEARING THINGS!

You are together for a reason. What's going on in your head and your heart is exactly what this relationship is based upon.

*I subscribe to Susan Scott's instruction not just to trust your instincts but also to obey them. In her outstanding book **Fierce Conversations** she pushes for each of us to listen to our internal radar. When the little hairs go up on the back of your neck, listen to them. When the knots in your stomach tighten, tune yourself in. When your trick shoulder dances a little out of place, let it lead.*

Tell your protégé what you are feeling. Ask her to comment on your feeling. You might say: "It seems to me that you are trying to have it both ways; can you see how I'd feel that way?" Or, "It's frustrating for me to see that you know what to do and you just don't do it; what's holding you back?"

If you are uncomfortable speaking up right now, ask permission. "While you were speaking a little voice inside me demanded some attention; may I share it with you?" Then say it! Don't mince words. Avoid the temptation to circle around a difficult subject hoping he will intuit what you mean.

Check in with yourself regularly – there's no "formula" to mentoring. There's more than one right way to do things, more than one right answer. The right way is the way that works for both of you – the protégé and the mentor. That's the approach to the questions the mentor asks of him or herself. Keep the end result in mind.

Where do you want to go, and will the choice you're making suit the goal? Mentoring is all about results; it's essential to ponder that question every time – and the answer is not the same for every protégé. Mentoring is not driven by YOUR style – you can't use the same style with every protégé.

Perhaps an example will help to illustrate this. I was mentoring a young woman and we were in conversation about her future in her family's business. Her dream was to be one of the Top 40 Under 40 leaders in Canada (this is a very prestigious designation). This was a dream she could accomplish so I asked her to write the speech she would give when she received the award six to eight years down the road. Her speech was exceptional. Her next task was to draw out some intermediate goals that would lead her to her dream and to identify how she would track those goals to measure progress.

When we next met, she was stuck. She couldn't think of her dream in those terms, and as we were talking, it dawned on me that she doesn't think in bullets, or tasks – she thinks in prose. So rather than asking her to write goals, I asked her to write the speech that, in a few years, her father would give as he turned the company over to her. In writing that speech, it became clear what her goals would be – these were the things we would work on.

I was giving her work that didn't suit her style – and it became too difficult for her; frustration set in. No one wants frustration. So I changed the task to suit her style. My style would be to list goals and tasks; she needed the sense of prose and story to do the work. So - not my way, but her way. It's her success on which we are focused.

When you think you know where you should go – go one step higher and take a look down. If I think my protégé needs direction – I'll look for something he needs to learn that would give him direction. I'm not so quick to go where my protégé thinks he wants to go. I pause and take a look, coming at it from the top, rather than from below.

Each of the mentor's roles builds on another, like a hierarchy or a ladder. So when we move from one to another, we need to look down from above to get perspective on our movement up until now. All the while, remember who is doing the work – don't let your protégé become dependent on you, or defer to you. They will, if you let them. Be their support, but don't be their doing. I see this in family businesses all the time. I hear comments like, "If only the kids will take more initiative!" Yet the children can't take initiative because as soon as it looks like they're heading for a mistake, the parents jump in to save them. As long as the kids are saved, they'll never have to learn to do it themselves.

Have Faith

A mentor needs to have faith. Faith means not knowing what's going to happen, but being prepared to live in whatever happens. If I knew what would happen, I wouldn't need faith, and I wouldn't be stretching. Even when you know that your protégé might not know, you can't give it all to them. He has to stretch to learn. Your job is to help him to live in ambiguity while having faith.

What has passed is history. In the future is vision. And the present creates the future – how you show up today determines what's unprecedented. When you live in the past or live in the future, you are distracted from the provision that you can be right now! We are human "be"ings. Honor your protégé by being with him, and only him. Stay in the conversation.

TIP   HOW FAR SHOULD I GO?

Ask one more question.

When the hair goes up on the back of your neck and you feel like you've reached a line, ask one more question. It is here that the resistance crumbles and the growth begins.

The Future is in Your Hands

Here ends our journey, my friend. I hope your travels have been safe and that you find yourself whole, affirmed, edified.

There are many ways of doing things; many paths leading to the same destination. You will be asked to lead the journey – it doesn't really matter which path you decide to take. Mentoring is who you are not what you're doing. Whatever advice you give, what will be remembered and valued is the passion, commitment and love with which you acted while you were giving.

Remember the one thing you can rely on is your intuition, and your intuition comes from knowledge and wisdom. Knowledge comes from learning – that' why you were willing to journey with me through this book. And wisdom comes from experience. That experience is yours to acquire through your own travels.

Mentoring is a gift, and a huge responsibility. For whom much is given, much is expected. You have been blessed with the ability to see what others don't, to go where others won't. Use it wisely and with great care and consideration. People are depending on you.

Dear Journal:

Now I'm in a pickle! Andy wants to formalize this process within his organization. He's so pleased with the way it's worked for him that he wants the up and coming folks in his organization to have a similar experience.

That's the good news.

The bad news is: he wants me to create and implement the process! What do I know about formalized mentoring programs? I only know who I am and what I do! Can I really teach a whole organization to do what I do? That will take a culture shift, for sure!

Still, I sure do know the rules about who mentors whom, and how to measure progress. And I understand the consequences of making mentoring a remedial program - no way would I let that happen!

So what will my most important message be? Someone I know once said that the best person to mentor is someone whose fortune and success are not dependent upon the success of the person being mentored. The investment, therefore, is strictly philanthropic - out of interest and commitment, and not expectation of future reward.

The other piece of wisdom I recall is that a mentor is one who pushes the protégé high, and when he lets go, there are no fingerprints on the person being lifted up to new heights. That is to say, none of me is left on the other - they are truly themselves and are of their own creation. They cannot be identified as copies of the original. They are the originals.

So, I think I will continue on this journey of mentorship. And be grateful to Andy for encouraging me to take the first step.

Afterword

Leaving a Legacy
"A Mentoring Organization"

In the past, mentoring has occurred on an ad hoc basis. An individual perhaps discovers she is stuck, momentum has stopped, and somewhere, somehow, she needs to get advice. So she scans friends, colleagues, acquaintances and role models to find the person who can provide the best advice. Lo and behold, a mentoring relationship is born. Most mentoring relationships are informal, and some are even serendipitous in the way they are established. Regardless of how the mentoring relationship develops, the truth is, mentoring works.

Many enlightened organizations have concluded that mentoring is an effective way of building future leaders. Predictably, many of those organizations are tempted to formalize the process. My fear is that in the business of creating a formal structure, the magic will be lost. If an organization wishes to create a mentoring environment, there are some hazards that need to be identified and avoided. Structurally, these groups need to understand how mentors are created, how to make the best matches and how to measure progress.

Agenda Matters

Starting at the beginning: what is the purpose for creating mentoring relationships within the organization, what outcomes does the organization anticipate and expect?

Right away you can see why I believe that a "mentoring organization" is not a viable concept

Obviously, a corporate mentoring structure is about using the mentoring process to the organization's advantage to artificially create enhanced performance for the primary benefit of the collective goals, likely the bottom line.

However, I fully support a corporation or agency that wishes to become an "organization of mentors".

The primary focus of an organization of mentors is personal and professional development of their people. Organizational, even bottom line, benefit would be a strategic byproduct of the mentoring process but not its intent. The primary aim is to develop the employee, the staff member, the leader into being the best they can be. Measurable results are an expected and welcome fringe benefit!

Consider whose agenda takes precedence – the organization's or the employee's? Whose interest is this relationship serving?

When the organization is clear the mentoring process is focused on the employee and his development, the climate is right for a mentoring model.

Four Questions

An organization about to embark on creating a mentoring environment has four questions to consider:

1.   Why would you do this?

Is this process for the employee or for management? Is this a method of valuing the employee, creating a nurturing environment, one that assists the individual to optimize their potential? The healthiest organizations are those in which each person feels they are in the right place at the right time. And this can't be static. The right place today may not be the right place tomorrow or next month or next year. If the employee is conscious of the importance of today, they will be happier, more focused and more productive, and are likely to create an environment that will be the right place for a longer period of time.

An organization focused on the health, motivation and productivity of its employees will create long-term, stable and consistent performance. If it's about the employee, the results will be win-win. If it's about the bottom line, eventually the protégé will begin to feel pressured and used. Serve the employee and everyone wins.

2. What is the platform for mentoring – career and/or life?

In a mentoring relationship, career and life are inextricably intertwined. Seeking success in one's career inevitably turns one to look inward, upward, and outward to the other aspects of life. The problem is that we take ourselves everywhere we go. You who profess that your work life is separate from your home life, which is separate from your social life are fooling yourselves, because there's a common denominator – you! If an organization intends to restrict mentoring relationships to a career focus, it does a grave disservice to the mentoring process. Mentoring is holistic – every aspect of life is involved. Be ready to shine that spotlight into the darkest, cobwebbed corners of life.

3. How will you match the people?

Mentoring cannot be mandated. People can be assigned to talk to each other, and if a relationship develops, that's great. If it doesn't – well, it doesn't and can't be forced. The process simply won't work without rapport between the mentor and the protégé. The protégé must want to find his own future, and must see that he is better able to get there with some help from one who has traveled farther down the road. The mentor must want to help another person clarify his own values, sense his own mission and embark on an intentional journey to accomplish his vision.

This is why a mentor can't be a supervisor – a supervisor is, and should be, concerned about results and outcomes. She has to, but doesn't want to, deal with the consequences of mistakes, so she's not prepared to live with mistakes. A mentor can encourage mistakes in the spirit of fostering and imprinting growth. A supervisor, given a choice, would choose productivity over growth. We have success by relying on experience, and we get experience by making mistakes. The mentor is a softer landing space.

The best way to set up a mentoring relationship is as follows:
- Determine which senior people are willing to invest in younger workers.
- Let potential protégés know who might be available as mentors.
- Make the process open for either party to approach the other with a request for a 15-minute conversation.
- In that conversation, search for compatibility and challenge – not goals and process. Can we talk with each other? Is there enough connection in our individual stories to make us want to spend time together? Search for differences, not just similarities; remember the goal is to challenge each other to higher levels, not just to rein force the current path. Your journey may do that; I just don't want you to approach it as if it's the only option. Thus my suggestion about mentoring from points of difference.
- Do you or can you evolve to trust each other? As we've said before, trust is essential to the relationship between mentor and protégé.
- Agree to another meeting with a set date and time.

4. What should we watch for?

As we said before, supervisors cannot mentor their direct reports. There's too much potential for mischief, confused agendas and misunderstandings. It is not possible to establish the level of trust required for a mentoring relationship. The best mentors are those for whom the success of the protégé has no impact on the mentor or his or her career. It should be arm's length. And confidentiality is an issue – it's impossible to keep confidences if there is an authority relationship between the two parties. The mentor does not need to be put in a position where necessary action must be taken – it's better when an objective, arm's-length mentor can coach the protégé into the appropriate action.

The mentoring process cannot be a belly-aching session about the protégé's current job or assignment. In fact, the mentor needs to remind the protégé that this process is about growth, not just about current reality or challenges. At times, the mentor may have to assist the protégé in preparing for a difficult conversation with her boss, but confidentiality goes both ways.

There is no chart, no structure for who should mentor whom; the connecting lines travel all over the organizational map.

Human Resource departments ought to provide training to potential mentors on the subject of mentoring to keep the process pure and duplicable. I suggest that HR thoroughly discuss the roles outlined here with their mentors, then follow up to check in. Are the mentors able to change hats smoothly – to switch from role to role – worker to mentor and back again? Even mentors need support and HR (or the mentoring champion within the organization) can provide encouragement, coaching, support and challenge to the managers engaged in mentoring.

And through it all, don't lose sight of the goals of the mentoring process. The focus is not measurable results for the organization, but the personal and professional growth of the employees who know their destination, are finding their path, and are discovering how their world today is helping to get them there.

An organization that creates an environment for mentoring does more than establish a climate for success. An organization of mentors creates a legacy for future executives, managers, employees, and their families – an unprecedented legacy of striving, risking and excellence in every part of life.

Appendix A
Self-Assessment Instruments

Meyers Briggs

A powerful and versatile indicator of personality type. Widely used for individual, group and organizational development. Revised for even greater accuracy and relevance. The MBTI® describes an individual's preferences on four dimensions; Extroverted vs. Introverted, Sensing vs. Intuitive, Thinking vs. Feeling, Judging vs. Perceiving. Individual Development – Identifying leadership style, developing managerial potential, time and stress management, and executive coaching

Kolbe Conative Index

Human instinct is the power behind our actions. It's the source of our mental (Conative) energy. Assessment tools have historically focused on measuring the cognitive (IQ) and the affective (person- ality) parts of the mind. While these tools are helpful in selecting, training and managing people, something has been missing. The Kolbe method allows you to maximize organizational performance by freeing people to utilize their instinctive talent and harnessing that talent in synergistic ways to productivity.

Strengthsfinder Profile

Performance management for organizations: People progress more rapidly in their areas of greatest talent than in their areas of weakness. Yet too many training and development approaches focus on making improvements in areas of weakness. Gallup takes the opposite approach. Gallup helps organizations capitalize on human talents through learning and developmental programs that show employees how to develop talents into strengths, then apply strengths to build personal and career success.

DISC Personality Profile

The DISC Classic Profile is a self-administered, self-scored, personal behavior assessment. Behavioral styles are grouped in four categories and the participant is guided through an in-depth interpretation of results. The instrument then provides feedback for building on strengths and increasing effectiveness in particular situations. The DISC Classic Profile enables individuals to:

Assess personal behaviour across four dimensions: dominance, influence, steadiness and conscientiousness

Discover their personal behavioural strengths and identify the environment conducive to their success

Learn about the differences of others and the environment they require for maximum productivity and teamwork

Leadership Practices Inventory (LPI)

The LPI is a 360-degree assessment instrument provides an assessment of individual leader's capacity in each of the five leadership practices detailed by Kouzes and Posner in **The Leadership Challenge:** Model the Way, Inspire a Shared Vision, Challenge the Process, Enable Others to Act, and Encourage the Heart.

It's simple: thirty behavioural statements that takes 20 minutes to complete. Leaders rate themselves on each of the thirty behaviours. Then, a handful of colleagues (manager, co-worker or peer, direct report) do the same thing relating their observations of the leader and his/her behaviour anonymously.

This data is highly valuable to assist, motivate and support a leader to improve his or her effectiveness.

EQ Assessment

Depending on the research, studies indicate that approximately 1-20% of life success comes from our intellectual intelligence (IQ) and the other 80-99% comes from other factors. Many of these others factors relate to how emotionally and socially literate we are as we work to achieve our view of success and fulfillment.

The need to be emotionally smart is particularly important during emotionally charged times: those times when we feel fearful, frustrated, and fatigued - fearful of workplace or relationship uncertainty, frustrated at having lost our "voice" and our sphere of influence, and fatigued from dealing with unrelenting workplace, career, relationship, and wellness challenges.

In order to effectively address these situations, individuals need to know how to get and keep themselves grounded, centred, and focused so they are not overwhelmed or blindsided by what is happening to them. Further, they need to ensure they are being emotionally grounded as they conduct their affairs, relate to a broad range of people, and make decisions that will affect them far into the future.

Wonderlic IQ Assessment

Used by a variety of employers, the Wonderlic Personnel Test (WPT) is a general test of problem solving ability that many consider to be the best measure of intelligence. The WPT provides indicators of an individual's ability to cope with the complexities of any particular occupation. The general consensus among psychologists is that cognitive ability--as tested on the Wonderlic--is the most reliable predictor of an individual's professional performance.

Appendix B
Recommended Reading

Beneath the Armor, Ole Carlson, Xlibris Corporation 2004
ISBN: 1413444350

Blink, Malcolm Gladwell, Little, Brown and Company 2005
ISBN: 0316172324 2005

Communication Catalyst, Connelly and Rianoshek, Dearborn
Publishing 2002 ISBN: 0793149045

Difficult Conversations, Stone, Patton, Heen, Guinness
Publishing 2000 ISBN: 014028852X

Fierce Conversations, Susan Scott, Berkley Trade 2003
ISBN: 0425193373

Good to Great, Jim Collins, Harper Collins 2001 Harper
Publishing ISBN: 0066620996

How Full is Your Bucket?, Rath and Clifton, Gallup 2004
ISBN: 1595620036

Inspire!, Lance Secretan, Wiley 2004 ISBN: 0471648825

Leadership and The Art of Self-Deception, Arbinger Institute,
Berrett-Koehler Publishing February 2002 ISBN: 157651740

Let Your Life Speak, Parker Palmer, Jossey-Bass Publishers 1999
ISBN: 0787947350

Now Discover Your Strengths, Marcus Buckingham, Free Press
2001 ISBN: 0743201140

Primal Leadership: Realizing the Power of Emotional
Intelligence, Daniel Goleman, Richard Boyatzis, Annie McKee,
Harvard Business School Press 2002 ISBN: 157851486X

7 Habits of Highly Effective People, Stephen Covey, Fireside
Publishing 1989 ISBN: 0-671-70863-5

Solving Tough Problems: An Open Way of Talking, Listening &
Creating New Realities, Adam Kahane, Berrett-Koehler
Publishing 2004 ISBN: 1576752933

The Art of Possibility, Benjamin & Rosamund Zander, Penguin
Publishing 2002 ISBN: 0142001104

The Contrarian's Guide to Leadership, Steven Sample, John Wiley
& Sons Canada 2003 ISBN: 0787967076

The Leadership Challenge, James Kouzes & Barry Posner, John
Wiley & Sons Canada 2003 ISBN: 0787968331

Tuesday's With Morrie, Mitch Albom, Doubleday 1977
ISBN: 076790592

When Generations Collide: Who They Are. Why They Clash.
How to Solve the Generational Puzzle at Work, Lynne Lancaster,
Harper Collins 2003 ISBN: 0066621070

Corey Olynik

"Helping individuals become more gives me energy," says Corey Olynik co-founder of **Executive Directions**, an innovative capacity-building initiative for not-for-profit leaders. "The most exciting thing about my work is the expectation that I will ask the tough questions, and look underneath the surface rooting out causes for personal and organizational logjams. Then, I get to watch the breakthroughs."

A full-time mentor, speaker and leadership coach, Corey walks with a variety of successful leaders. "I've worked with achievers in a number of different venues: entrepreneurs, political figures, not-for-profit leaders. Most find themselves trapped 'in their organization' and unable to work 'on their organization.' Helping people make that transition (that leap!) is my passion."

Corey's background includes time in the private, public and non-profit sectors. A former broadcast executive, pastor and strategic advisor to senior political leaders, he knows first-hand what it's like to wrestle with the short and long-term challenges leaders face.

Corey and his wife Kathleen live in Calgary, Alberta. They have two grown sons.

Contact Corey at:

www.coreyolynik.com
info@coreyolynik.com
(403) 269-1117